GOD'S WORD, GOD'S WORLD... and YOU

A FRESH LOOK AT EVANGELISM

From the Bible-teaching ministry of

CHARLES R. SWINDOLL

INSIGHT FOR LIVING

Chuck graduated in 1963 from Dallas Theological Seminary, where he now serves as the school's fourth president, helping to prepare a new generation of men and women for the ministry. Chuck has served in pastorates in three states: Massachusetts, Texas, and California, including almost twenty-three years at the First Evangelical Free Church in Fullerton, California. His sermon messages have been aired over radio since 1979 as the *Insight for Living* broadcast. A best-selling author, Chuck has written numerous books and booklets on many subjects.

Based on the outlines and transcripts of Chuck's sermons, the study guide text is co-authored by Bryce Klabunde, a graduate of Biola University and Dallas Theological Seminary. He also wrote the Living Insights sections.

Editor in Chief:
Cynthia Swindoll

Graphics System Administrator:
Bob Haskins

Coauthor of Text:
Bryce Klabunde

Director, Communications Division:
John Norton

Assistant Editor and Writer:
Wendy Peterson

Project Coordinator:
Colette Muse

Copy Editor:
Karene Wells

Print Production Manager:
Don Bernstein

Text Designer:
Gary Lett

Printer:
Sinclair Printing Company

Unless otherwise identified, all Scripture references are from the New American Standard Bible, © The Lockman Foundation 1960, 1962, 1963, 1968, 1971, 1972, 1973, 1975, 1977. Used by permission. Other translations cited are *The Living Bible* [LB] and *The New Testament in Modern English* [PHILLIPS].

An effort has been made to locate sources and obtain permission where necessary for the quotations used in this book. In the event of any unintentional omission, a modification will gladly be incorporated in future printings.

ISBN 0-8499-9951-0
COVER PHOTOGRAPH: *Philippe the Deacon Baptises the Eunuch of the Queen of Ethiopia*, Church of Saint Roch, Chapel/Explorer, Paris. By permission of SuperStock, Inc.
COVER DESIGN: Gary Lett
Printed in the United States of America

CONTENTS

INTRODUCTION

*E*vangelism is tracts, crusades, and altar calls. It's door-to-door witnessing. Tuesday night visitation. Revivals.

At least, that's what we often assume.

Actually, evangelism is much broader than those techniques . . . much bigger than a once-a-year event or a weekly program. It's both natural and supernatural. It includes both simple conversations and life-changing conversions. It's as complex as the relationships it flows out of and as diverse as the people it reaches. Through the gospel it proclaims, evangelism is God's channel of love to a lost and needy world.

I'm so glad you've chosen to take a fresh look at evangelism with me. I promise you, this won't be a "ten steps to successful soul winning"-type Bible study. As helpful as good techniques are, I've decided to focus this study on things like prayer and attitudes and lifestyles and perspectives—the heart of the Christian. Because that's where true evangelism begins.

Chuck Swindoll

Chuck Swindoll

PUTTING TRUTH
INTO ACTION

Knowledge apart from application falls short of God's desire for
His children. He wants us to apply what we learn so that we
will change and grow. This study guide was prepared with these
goals in mind. As you go through the following pages, we hope your
desire to discover biblical truth will grow as your understanding of
God's Word increases and that you will be encouraged to apply what
you've learned.

To assist you in your study, we've included a section called
Living Insights at the end of each lesson. These exercises will
challenge you to study further and to think of specific ways
to put your discoveries into action.

There are many ways to use this guide—in personal devotions,
group studies, discussions with friends and family, and Sunday school
classes. And, of course, it's an ideal study aid when you're listening
to its corresponding *Insight for Living* radio series.

To benefit most from this study guide, we would encourage you
to consider it a spiritual journal. That's why we've included space
in the **Living Insights** for recording your thoughts and discoveries.
We hope you'll return to those sections often for review and en-
couragement as you continue to grow in your walk with Christ.

Bryce Klabunde

Bryce Klabunde
Coauthor of Text
Author of Living Insights

God's Word, God's World . . . and You

A FRESH LOOK AT EVANGELISM

Chapter 1

GOD'S STRANGE CHANGE PLAN

Selected Scriptures

Jean Valjean felt no remorse as he slipped the gleaming silverware in his pocket. Although the kind bishop had fed and sheltered him, he needed cash, and the bishop's silver would fetch a handsome price. After all, considering what society had done to him, why should he think of anyone except himself?

Years earlier, he had stolen a loaf of bread to feed his starving niece. Caught in the act, he had been slapped in irons and sentenced to hard labor. For nineteen years, he had toiled on a chain gang, his back bearing the full force of the whip of the law. When finally paroled, he emerged a hardened and hateful man. He had taken a loaf of bread, but society had stolen his self-respect. As an ex-con, he was condemned to a life of destitution and disgrace. The silverware was small repayment for the scars he bore.

Unfortunately, the police didn't see it that way. When they found the silverware on him, they dragged him to the bishop to return the stolen goods before throwing him back in prison. However, in a moving display of mercy, the bishop told the police that the silverware was a gift and offered Valjean two costly candlesticks to take as well.

Astonished and overwhelmed by the bishop's response, Valjean felt the chains of bitterness fall away from his heart. Grace had done what the law could not—set him free to start a new life of compassion and generosity toward outcasts like himself.

You might recognize this dramatic scene from Victor Hugo's

1

novel *Les Miserables*, which was beautifully adapted for the theater. In the story, the bishop symbolizes God, and Valjean represents us. Like him, we stand condemned, our sin fully exposed and deserving judgment. But with a surprising twist, God abundantly pardons us. As the prophet Isaiah tells us:

> Seek the Lord while He may be found;
> Call upon Him while He is near.
> Let the wicked forsake his way,
> And the unrighteous man his thoughts;
> And let him return to the Lord,
> And He will have compassion on him;
> And to our God,
> For He will abundantly pardon. (Isa. 55:6–7)

Why would He do that? In some ways, the reason is a mystery. The Lord explains it best:

> "My thoughts are not your thoughts,
> Neither are your ways My ways," declares the Lord.
> "For as the heavens are higher than the earth,
> So are My ways higher than your ways,
> And My thoughts than your thoughts." (vv. 8–9)

God operates on a higher plane than we do, and His ways are strange to us. And here is the starting point of any study on evangelism: God's method of changing the world is unlike anything we could imagine. If we are going to be His witnesses, we must first learn to appreciate His strange and sometimes startling ways.

God's Ways versus Our Ways

Reflecting on the life of Christ, we can see at least six examples of how God's ways are strange to us.

A Strange Incarnation Plan

Let's begin with the incredible account of the Virgin Birth (see Matt. 1:18–25). Who would have thought that the Son of God would make His royal entrance into the world through the womb of an unknown, unmarried peasant girl. From our point of view, it's scandalous. From God's perspective, it's perfect. By creating life within a virgin, the Holy Spirit protected the tiny embryo from sin. Adam's curse could not touch Jesus. Because of the Virgin Birth,

He could be the fully human and fully divine Lamb of God to atone for the sins of the world (see Rom. 5:12, 17–21).

A Strange Assortment of Messengers

When it came time for Jesus to start His ministry, whom did God choose to launch Him on His way?

> Now in those days John the Baptist came, preaching in the wilderness of Judea, saying, "Repent, for the kingdom of heaven is at hand." (Matt. 3:1–2)

In modern terms, John was a marketing nightmare. His style was offensive; his message, negative; and his appearance . . . well, just look at him!

> Now John himself had a garment of camel's hair, and a leather belt about his waist; and his food was locusts and wild honey. (v. 4)

Not the sort of front man we'd want endorsing us for public office. But Jesus wasn't a politician. He had a much grander purpose in mind, and John was the right man for the job. Was his unorthodox manner effective?

> Then Jerusalem was going out to him, and all Judea, and all the district around the Jordan. (v. 5)

John was just one of several unlikely people God chose to demonstrate His redemptive plan. Add to him the twelve disciples, among whom were two pairs of fishermen brothers, a tax collector, and a political zealot—as diverse a group of people as ever were assembled.

Humanly speaking, the disciples were woefully unqualified for their calling. Jesus was establishing a new spiritual order, a kingdom that would transcend ethnic boundaries and change the world. Surely He would need a team of influential movers and shakers— well-polished, highly skilled professionals. Yet the disciples had no political connections or university training. They were common people with common failings. Impulsive Peter often spoke first and thought later (see Matt. 16:21–23). Ambitious James and John tried to elbow their way to the top of the kingdom ladder (see Mark 10:35–41). And even though the Twelve traveled with Jesus for more than three years, they never quite grasped what He was teaching.

Would we have selected a group like that? Probably not. But

3

then, God's thoughts are not our thoughts. He looks at our hearts, not our resumés. For all their foibles, the disciples displayed one quality Jesus valued above all else—devotion to Him.

A Strange Response to Criticism

The legalistic Pharisees, however, despised Jesus. Offended by His grace-oriented ministry, they hurled stones of criticism at Him, as Jesus noted: "The Son of Man has come eating and drinking; and you say, 'Behold, a gluttonous man, and a drunkard, a friend of tax-gatherers and sinners!'" (Luke 7:34).

How did the Son of God respond to these attacks—and worse, being called in so many words "the son of Satan" (see Matt. 9:34)?

> And Jesus was going about all the cities and the villages, teaching in their synagogues, and proclaiming the gospel of the kingdom, and healing every kind of disease and every kind of sickness. (v. 35)

Unhindered by the hail of slander, Jesus marched forward in His ministry. Modern advisors would have counseled Jesus to counterattack. "Sue!" they would have urged Him. Jesus' way, however, is different from ours. More important things occupied His time and energy, like loving the lost.

A Strange Ministry Strategy

Out of the farms and villages, they came to Him by the thousands—the sick, the hungry, the broken, the dying—each of them reaching to Christ for help. From a purely business point of view, Jesus' popularity was an oil well of opportunity. Seeing the crowds, we might have tugged on Jesus' tunic, "It's time to strike while the iron is hot. Let's put a sales team together, print up some T-shirts, publish some books."

But when Jesus saw the multitudes, He

> felt compassion for them, because they were distressed and downcast like sheep without a shepherd. Then He said to His disciples, "The harvest is plentiful, but the workers are few. Therefore beseech the Lord of the harvest to send out workers into His harvest." (vv. 36–38)

Instead of a marketing strategy, Jesus developed a prayer strategy. Because when we pray, we stop counting numbers. We focus on the task at hand—getting the crops in—not on who reaps the most cash and converts. And we focus on God, the Lord of the harvest.

A Strange Method of Ministry

From the beginning, Jesus planned to equip others to carry on His work. He promised His disciples, "Follow Me, and I will make you fishers of men" (4:19). When the time was right, He handed them the net. But first, He gave them the one thing they would need before they could catch anyone.

> And having summoned His twelve disciples, He gave them authority over unclean spirits, to cast them out, and to heal every kind of disease and every kind of sickness. (10:1)

Rather than loading them down with a three-inch evangelism training manual, five videotapes, and a box of tracts, He gave them His badge of authority to act in His name. No power on earth or in heaven could stand against that. Then He delineated the boundaries of their ministry:

> These twelve Jesus sent out after instructing them, saying, "Do not go in the way of the Gentiles, and do not enter any city of the Samaritans; but rather go to the lost sheep of the house of Israel." (vv. 5–6)

Next He gave them the words to say:

> "And as you go, preach, saying, 'The kingdom of heaven is at hand.'" (v. 7)

And He outlined their primary tasks:

> "Heal the sick, raise the dead, cleanse the lepers, cast out demons; freely you received, freely give." (v. 8)

Finally, He spelled out their code of conduct:

> "Do not acquire gold, or silver, or copper for your money belts, or a bag for your journey, or even two tunics, or sandals, or a staff; for the worker is worthy of his support. And into whatever city or village you enter, inquire who is worthy in it; and abide there

until you go away. And as you enter the house, give it your greeting. And if the house is worthy, let your greeting of peace come upon it; but if it is not worthy, let your greeting of peace return to you. And whoever does not receive you, nor heed your words, as you go out of that house or that city, shake off the dust of your feet. Truly I say to you, it will be more tolerable for the land of Sodom and Gomorrah in the day of judgment, than for that city." (vv. 9–15)

Can you imagine anyone today signing up for a no-pay, no-perks job like that? Moving from town to town. Never sure of your welcome. It's certainly not our way, is it?

A Strange Plan of Protection

When we offer people a job, we usually try to paint an attractive picture for them. We tour them through the plush, oak-trimmed hallways; we invite them to the company health club; we drive them along the tree-lined streets of the suburbs where they might live.

When Jesus hired His disciples, he sketched this realistic picture:

"Behold, I send you out as sheep in the midst of wolves; therefore be shrewd as serpents, and innocent as doves. But beware of men; for they will deliver you up to the courts, and scourge you in their synagogues. . . . And you will be hated by all on account of My name, but it is the one who has endured to the end who will be saved." (vv. 16–17, 22)

Jesus doesn't sugarcoat the life of a disciple to gain recruits. We might try to hide the negatives in fine print, but He puts them in bold type. At the same time, He consistently urges us, "Do not fear" (vv. 26, 28, 31). After pointing us down such a terrifying path, how can He say this? Because along with the promise of pain comes His guarantee of divine justice (v. 26) and of our infinite value to God, who watches over even the sparrows (vv. 29–31).

What Are We to Make of All This?

The One who devised so many "strange" strategies and methods is the same One who sends us out with the equally outrageous command: "Go therefore and make disciples of all the nations" (28:19). Can you imagine how impossible it must have sounded to

6

the ragtag assortment of disciples who first heard it? Questioning glances must have shot around the group, "Us? Take on the world?"

Yet within a generation, the grassroots movement of Christianity had spread throughout the Roman Empire, reaching even the guards in Caesar's palace (see Phil. 1:12–13). Today, Christ places His crazy, world-changing mission in our hands. If we desire to be a part of it, we must be prepared to go about it His way. Practically, that means four things:

- *We must learn to be comfortable with the unusual.* God may use methods of evangelism that seem strange to us, but we must be willing to break our molds to fit His style.

- *We must be open to the unrehearsed.* God keeps us on our toes! He delights in the spontaneous. If our carefully laid plans go awry, God may be setting a new opportunity for the gospel that we never anticipated.

- *We must be ready for the disapproval of others.* If the world rejected God's Son, it will also reject us. Count on it.

- *We must be weary of being dissatisfied.* God is looking for Christians who long to get out of the religious rut—people who yearn to try something fresh and unusual. Is that you? Are you willing to let go of the ordinary to reach out for the extraordinary? Then you're ready to join God's way and reach the world.

 Living Insights

The scene is heaven. The Son of God is sitting on His glorious throne, strategizing with His angels about how He will rescue humankind from the enemy.

"Here's the plan. I slip into the pool of humanity as a helpless baby and let thirty years pass without a ripple. Then I emerge as a humble teacher, traveling by foot and relying on the handouts of My followers. For about three years, I touch the untouchables, rub shoulders with sinners, and pour My treasure of eternal truth into the callused hands of unschooled disciples.

"Then, at the climax of My earthly life, I surrender Myself to the Prince of Darkness and allow evil men to brutalize and murder Me. A shadow of despair blackens the earth for three days. On the third day, I break death's grip and rise from the grave victorious! But, instead of unveiling Myself as a conquering hero, I peek in to see My most faithful followers, then quietly ascend to heaven. Before I leave, I entrust My story to a huddled group of apprehensive believers and tell them to use it to win the world.

"Well . . . what do you think?"

———————◆———————

If you were one of the angels, how would you respond? What part of His plan seems the most amazing to you?

_____

_____

_____

Perhaps the greatest lesson we can learn from this study is this: You can't put Christ in a box. You can't say, "He only works this way." Because He will go to the most incredible lengths and do the most unexpected things to save people.

There's a lot to consider before we sign up to work for Christ. If we're serious about our commitment to Him, our lives may take a drastic and unexpected turn.

Knowing that Christ's ways are different from ours, are you prepared to be His messenger? Are you flexible enough to follow His way of doing things even if it takes you beyond your level of comfort?

Those questions may require some thought before answering. Take your time. When you're ready, express your response in the form of a pledge to Christ.

My Pledge

_____

_____

_____

_____

_____

_____

_____

Chapter 2

SHARING THE GOOD NEWS AS A CHURCH

Survey of Acts

I magine that you were a member of a church during its early days,
before it grew into a large ministry . . .

Back then, you didn't have much—no property, no building,
and not a lot of money. But you had a dream of reaching the
community for Christ, and that was all you needed.

Remember meeting in that old, drafty trailer? The first Bible
club in the park? Canvassing neighborhoods? The work was tiring,
and sometimes you felt like giving up. But the Lord honored each
faltering step of faith, and soon the fruit began to emerge.

Every Sunday, new people came, and the sapling church began
to grow lush and green. Services were moved to the high school
gymnasium. A piano was donated, along with folding chairs and a
PA system. You could see the Lord changing lives.

What a day it was when you broke ground for your own building!
And as the sanctuary went up, even more people flowed in. So you
hired additional staff, went to multiple services, and added a wide
array of ministries.

Now on Sundays, people enjoy fine Christian music and solid
biblical preaching. The church offers more programs than you can
count: small groups, midweek children's programs, camps, mission
trips, even exercise classes.

The church is a success. But along with great success comes an
equally great danger: *complacency*.

As a church expands, its original mission can get lost in the
dusty pile of building scraps. When the construction is finally finished, the passion to evangelize is often swept aside as people settle
into their favorite programs. The hard work has been done. The
church is full. Our needs are being met. Why reach out?

Evangelism, however, isn't just a tool to get a church up and
running. It isn't a booster rocket that launches the ship into space,
then falls away once it's in orbit. The drive to save the lost must
continually energize the church . . . just like it energized the early
church in the book of Acts.

Spreading the Flame

Acts is the compelling story of how Christianity spread from a tiny flame to a worldwide blaze. The book's theme verse, Acts 1:8, sketches a map of the gospel's path as it fanned outward from Jerusalem:

> "But you shall receive power when the Holy Spirit
> has come upon you; and you shall be My witnesses
> both in Jerusalem, and in all Judea and Samaria, and
> even to the remotest part of the earth."

The early church never lost sight of this vision. Wherever the first believers went, they proclaimed the good news of salvation— first in Jerusalem, then in the surrounding regions of Judea and Samaria, and finally in the far reaches of the world.

Do you want to see how they did it? Then strap on your boots, and let's follow the early Christians as they spread the flame of Christ through their world.

In Jerusalem

The initial burst of evangelism took place in Jerusalem on the Day of Pentecost. The Holy Spirit had ignited a small group of believers with power (just as Jesus had promised), when Peter stood up to proclaim the gospel to the Jewish crowds. By the end of the day, the church had grown from about a hundred members to about three thousand (Acts 2:41)!

Can you imagine starting a church with three thousand baby believers? The apostles certainly had their hands full. The first task was to feed them a diet rich in spiritual protein:

> And they were continually devoting themselves to
> the apostles' teaching and to fellowship, to the
> breaking of bread and to prayer.
> And everyone kept feeling a sense of awe; and
> many wonders and signs were taking place through
> the apostles. (vv. 42–43)

Well-nourished on fellowship, biblical teaching, and prayer, the believers started growing by leaps and bounds. Eagerly, they shared their possessions and worshiped the Lord together (vv. 44–46). Verse 47 says that they were "having favor with all the people." As a result, "the Lord was adding to their number day by day those who were being saved."

In chapter 4, Peter preached a second evangelistic message. This one got him arrested, but not before "many of those who had heard the message believed" (v. 4a). How many? "The number of the men came to be about five thousand" (v. 4b).

Amazing! Within weeks, the number of new Christians had grown larger than the population of many small cities. And as the apostles kept ministering and performing miracles in the temple, the numbers kept rising. "All the more believers in the Lord, multitudes of men and women, were constantly added to their number" (5:14).

At this point, the most serious threat to the expansion of the church came not from the outside but the inside. In the daily food disbursements, a certain group of needy widows were being neglected. Accusations of prejudice were splitting the seams of the church. The apostles held the assembly together by instructing the people to appoint deacons to oversee this ministry (see 6:1–6). Its unity preserved, the church could refocus on its mission to reach the lost:

> And the word of God kept on spreading; and the
> number of the disciples continued to increase greatly
> in Jerusalem, and a great many of the priests were
> becoming obedient to the faith. (v. 7)

Even the priests were turning to Christ. Can you imagine the headlines in the *Jerusalem Gazette?* "Priests Claim Crucified Nazarene Is Lamb of God." What a shock to the Jewish leaders, who thought they had rid themselves of the vexatious Jesus! Spread simply by people touching people, the grassroots movement had invaded the ranks of even the religious elite. A violent reaction loomed certain.

The clash occurred when Stephen was dragged before the Sanhedrin—the council that condemned Christ. In his defense statement, Stephen accused the white-robed leaders of murdering God's "Righteous One" (7:52). Snarling and gnashing their teeth, they rushed him like a pack of wolves, drove him out of the city, and stoned him to death.

In Judea and Samaria

Stephen's martyrdom opened the floodgates of persecution. Instead of smothering the gospel's flame, however, the persecution sent it streaming out of Jerusalem into Judea and Samaria. As the believers fled, they "went about preaching the word" (8:4). *Nothing* could

11

squelch their evangelistic zeal to tell others the good news of Christ.

Acts 9 records the conversion of Saul, the chief persecutor of Christianity, who later became Paul, its chief promoter. With his conversion, the church grew even more. Three verses in this chapter convey the spirit of expansion during this period:

> So the church throughout all Judea and Galilee and Samaria enjoyed peace, being built up; and, going on in the fear of the Lord and in the comfort of the Holy Spirit, it continued to increase. (v. 31)

Verse 35 adds this comment after Peter cured a paralytic in the city of Lydda:

> And all who lived at Lydda and Sharon saw him, and they turned to the Lord.

And when Peter raised Dorcas from the dead in Joppa, this was the response:

> And it became known all over Joppa, and many believed in the Lord. (v. 42)

Of course, we're not Peter, and we don't generally raise people from the dead. But we do not have to be Peter to share the gospel. Acts 11 records the evangelistic efforts of ordinary believers who had fled to Antioch during the persecution (see v. 19). When they arrived, they targeted just the Jews, but then some believers from Cyprus and Cyrene

> came to Antioch and began speaking to the Greeks also, preaching the Lord Jesus. And the hand of the Lord was with them, and a large number who believed turned to the Lord. (vv. 20–21)

Many Jews in the early church wanted to stamp the gospel "For Jews Only." The Christians in Antioch, however, opened it to everyone. It is fitting that this church at Antioch would become the new center of Christianity and the pad for launching the gospel into the remotest part of the earth.

To the Remotest Part of the Earth

Acts 13 marks the beginning of the final phase of Christ's mission to reach the world—a phase that is still in operation today. Selected by the Holy Spirit and commissioned by the church, Barnabas and

Saul set out on the first missionary journey. Their first stop: the island of Cyprus. Then they sailed across the sea to what is now southern Turkey. In city after city, they preached in the synagogues and established fledgling churches among the Gentiles. Retracing their steps, they returned to Antioch, glowing with reports of what God had done (see 14:26–28).

After parting ways with Barnabas, Saul (now called Paul) selected Silas as his traveling partner, and the pair hiked through Turkey. On and on they walked, hoping at every stopover for opportunities to speak the Word. But the Holy Spirit kept closing the doors (see 16:6–7). Finally, at Troas, they reached the end of the road. Stretching before them was the Aegean Sea and beyond that . . . Macedonia, Greece, and all of Europe. "What should we do, Lord?" Paul must have wondered. That night, God answered his prayer.

> And a vision appeared to Paul in the night: a certain man of Macedonia was standing and appealing to him, and saying, "Come over to Macedonia and help us." And when he had seen the vision, immediately we sought to go into Macedonia, concluding that God had called us to preach the gospel to them. (vv. 9–10)

The missionaries carried the flame to such cities as Philippi, Thessalonica, and Corinth. As the apostles traveled, they handed off the torch to the new believers. Later, when Paul circled back, he was delighted to discover the region ablaze with the light of the gospel. He proudly wrote to the Thessalonians:

> For the word of the Lord has sounded forth from you, not only in Macedonia and Achaia, but also in every place your faith toward God has gone forth, so that we have no need to say anything. (1 Thess. 1:8)

Whew! That's quite a whirlwind trip from Jerusalem to Macedonia, and we're not through yet. Paul will carry the gospel as far as Rome before the book ends. In a way, though, Acts never ends, for we are adding our own chapter today as we continue spreading the flame.

Spreading the Flame Today

The early Christians have a lot to teach us about evangelism. First, we can find a warning: *personal complacency is a major peril.* People can water down the name *Christian* to mean anyone who

13

attends church on Sundays. However, in the truest sense of the word, *Christian* means a follower of Christ—a person whose heart burns with the fire of Jesus and who yearns to carry His flame to the lost. The name implies a mission, a purpose, a direction in life. Without that sense of calling, we lose our identity as the people of God. We become just another social club with a religious-sounding name.

Second, we uncover an exhortation: *congregational commitment is the hope of our survival.* The church isn't designed to be an end in itself but a means to an end—that is, the redemption of the world. As long as one person doesn't know Christ, our work is not finished.

With a vision like that, we can't afford to fold our arms and let "the professionals" do the evangelism. We don't have the luxury of resting on the laurels of past successes. Every church, every member, every hand reaching the lost—that's our vision.

 Living Insights

God's heart beats with a passion to save the lost. From that first dark day when sin separated Him from His creation, He has been reaching out to humankind. "Where are you?" God called to Adam and Eve hiding themselves in shame. And, like a father searching for a lost child, He has been calling out to the world ever since.

He called out in the days of Noah, when He arched the rainbow in the sky as a symbol of hope.

He called out through Abraham and His promise that in him "all the families of the earth shall be blessed" (Gen. 12:3).

He called out through the Hebrew people, who marched on dry land through the waters of judgment as living illustrations of His redemptive power.

He called out through the tabernacle, when He funneled His glory into the Holy of Holies and offered atonement for sins in exchange for the blood of a lamb.

He called out through the prophets, who showed the way of genuine repentance and faith.

Finally, He called out through His Son, who made atonement on the cross and, three days later, conquered death once and for all.

Is God still calling to the world? You bet. But He doesn't speak through a temple or a nation; He speaks through us. We who believe in His Son are His megaphone through which He pleads with the world to be saved.

Is He speaking loud and clear through your life? Does your heart beat with God's passion for the lost?

All the evangelistic techniques we can devise are worthless if our hearts are complacent toward the unsaved. Do you struggle with complacency? How so?

_____

_____

_____

The same God who fanned the fire in the early Christians can ignite a blaze in you. Look up the following verses that demonstrate His passion for the lost. Then take a moment to tell Him that, more than anything, you want His heart to beat in you.

Ezekiel 33:11   1 Timothy 2:3–4

Matthew 9:35–38   2 Peter 3:9

_____

_____

_____

_____

_____

_____

Chapter 3

TAKING ADVANTAGE OF TODAY'S ADVANTAGES
Luke 10:25–37

There was a time when the earth must have seemed as vast as the universe. The notion of someone sailing across the ocean was as unlikely as one of us flying to Pluto. On old maps, uncharted regions included pictures of dragons and enchanted kingdoms. Early explorers spent years planning a thousand-mile journey and set out not knowing if they would ever return.

Today, though, the world doesn't seem so big and mysterious. We can jet a thousand miles in a couple of hours, conduct business, and make it home in time for dinner. We can watch via satellite a live update of an earthquake disaster halfway around the world. Through the Internet, we can strike up a conversation with strangers from South Africa, San Francisco, and Singapore. Or we can browse for rare books in a British bookshop, place an order, and have the package delivered in a scant few days.

Instead of a global universe, the world has indeed become a global village. And as the information superhighway speeds us into the future, we're fast on our way to becoming a global neighborhood.

Truly, the world is at our doorstep . . . or, at our fingertips. And as our circles of contact stretch farther and wider, we find ourselves within arm's reach of more and more hurting people. Whom should we care for? How can we share Christ's love with them? Now more than ever the question voiced by a Jewish lawyer to Jesus resounds with relevance: "Who is my neighbor?"

Addressing the Heart of the Issue

Rather than preach the answer, Jesus masterfully pictures it in the moving story of the Good Samaritan. The parable is set in the context of a conversation He is having with a Jewish lawyer who wanted to put Jesus to the test (Luke 10:25a).

This chapter is adapted from "What about My Neighbor's Neighbor?" from the study guide *The Continuation of Something Great: Jesus' Teaching and Training of the Disciples, A Study of Luke 7:1–10:37,* coauthored by Bryce Klabunde, from the Bible-teaching ministry of Charles R. Swindoll (Anaheim, Calif.: Insight for Living, 1995), pp. 130–35.

16

Dialogue . . . a Lawyer and Jesus

The legal expert begins the dialogue by asking a question,

> "Teacher, what shall I do to inherit eternal life?"
> (v. 25b)

Turning the test around, Jesus answers the man with another question:

> "What is written in the Law? How does it read to you?" (v. 26)

The key to eternal life is within the lawyer's grasp—literally. According to William Barclay,

> Strict orthodox Jews wore round their wrists little leather boxes called phylacteries, which contained certain passages of scripture—*Exodus* 13:1–10; 11–16; *Deuteronomy* 6:4–9; 11:13–20. . . . So Jesus said to the scribe, "Look at the phylactery on your own wrist and it will answer your question."[1]

Adding a phrase from Leviticus 19:18, the lawyer quotes the Scripture he has dutifully wrapped around his memory,

> "You shall love the Lord your God with all your heart, and with all your soul, and with all your strength, and with all your mind; and your neighbor as yourself." (Luke 10:27)

Jesus congratulates him for his right answer, but He also challenges the lawyer to go beyond Scripture memory and start putting his knowledge into action.

> And He said to him, "You have answered correctly; do this, and you will live." (v. 28)

Today we would say, "You got it. Now get at it!" As far as Jesus is concerned, the case is closed.

The lawyer, however, doesn't care for the incriminating verdict. So he tries to squirm off the hook of responsibility by quibbling over the meaning of a word.

---

1. William Barclay, *The Gospel of Luke,* rev. ed., The Daily Study Bible Series (Philadelphia, Pa.: Westminster Press, 1975), p. 140.

> But wishing to justify himself, he said to Jesus, "And who is my neighbor?" (v. 29)

Using an old debater's trick, the lawyer tries to win the argument by disorienting his opponent in a confusing maze of definitions. Some rabbis of the day, according to Barclay, "confined the word *neighbor* to their *fellow Jews.*"[2] What does Jesus think? Sidestepping the definitions debate, Jesus instead tells a story that explains His meaning beyond a doubt.

Monologue . . . Jesus and a Story

> Jesus replied and said, "A certain man was going down from Jerusalem to Jericho; and he fell among robbers, and they stripped him and beat him, and went off leaving him half dead." (v. 30)

Jesus' story is about a man in need—a man who had taken a treacherous journey from Jerusalem to Jericho. The route between those cities was craggy and steep, and the altitude dropped thirty-six hundred feet over a distance of twenty miles. Robbers loved that lonely stretch of road. They could mug, assault, and rape without fear of intervention. Called "The Bloody Way," it was a threatening, dangerous road for a person traveling alone.[3]

As Jesus continues, the drama heightens. He introduces two religious men into His story, drawing the pious lawyer into a net of emotional identification.

> "And by chance a certain priest was going down on that road, and when he saw him, he passed by on the other side. And likewise a Levite also, when he came to the place and saw him, passed by on the other side." (vv. 31–32)

A priest and a Levite, two religious professionals perhaps hurrying to perform their sacred duties, saw the man but ignored the need.

Jesus contrasts their response with that of another traveler—one despised by Jews, a Samaritan.

> "But a certain Samaritan, who was on a journey, came upon him; and when he saw him, he felt compassion,

---

2. Barclay, *The Gospel of Luke*, p. 140.

3. Barclay, *The Gospel of Luke*, pp. 138–39.

and came to him, and bandaged up his wounds, pouring oil and wine on them; and he put him on his own beast, and brought him to an inn, and took care of him. And on the next day he took out two denarii and gave them to the innkeeper and said, 'Take care of him; and whatever more you spend, when I return, I will repay you.'" (vv. 33–35)

Samaritans were Jews whose ancestors came from the northern ten tribes of Israel and who long ago had intermarried with the Assyrians. They held that Mount Gerizim, not Jerusalem, was the true place of worship. For these reasons, the full-blooded Jews looked down on the Samaritans and criticized their errant beliefs. Yet it was a Samaritan whose faith proved the most worthy.

Jesus says the Samaritan "felt compassion." He saw the same pitiful man lying in agony as the priest and Levite did, but his heart churned within him so that he couldn't pass by without helping. That's the way compassion affects us. It stirs us; it troubles us; it keeps us awake at night until we do something.

Did you notice the lengths to which the Samaritan went to show love to the man?

- he came to him
- he poured healing oil and wine on his wounds
- he bandaged them
- he put the man on his beast and brought him to an inn
- he took care of him through the night
- the next day, he made provisions for his recovery

Unlike Jerusalem's religious elite, the Samaritan went the extra mile for this man in need. He was a good neighbor—which brings Jesus to the point of His story.

Question . . . The Story and a Neighbor

Jesus narrows His message to a single question, thrust like a spear to its mark—the lawyer's heart.

"Which of these three do you think proved to be a neighbor to the man who fell into the robbers' hands?" And he said, "The one who showed mercy toward him." And Jesus said to him, "Go and do the same." (vv. 36–37)

The Lord deftly shifts the original question from "Who is my neighbor?" to the more important question, "What kind of neighbor am I?" Like the lawyer, we often want to place the burden of responsibility on someone else's shoulders. Our degree of mercy depends on whether people fit our definition of a worthy neighbor. But Jesus throws the burden back on us. He puts our prejudices to the test, particularly when He places someone of another culture on our path. The issue is not, Is my neighbor really lost? But, Are we—our neighbor's neighbors—really saved? Are we people of compassion, who love the Lord our God with all our heart, soul, strength, and mind . . . who love our neighbors as ourselves and prove it with our actions?

Coming to Terms with the Truth

The answer to that question depends on who we are and our desire to change, if necessary. Although three men observed the wounded traveler, only the Samaritan saw the man's brokenness and pain. Why? Because he had a heart of compassion. As a result, he bent down to help. The principle is this: Who we are determines what we see, and what we see determines what we do.

How do you see the wounded people along the ever-expanding highways of the world in which you travel? Christ tells us to view them with eyes of compassion and to reach out to them with hands of mercy. According to James, our faith isn't much good if we don't demonstrate it with loving deeds:

> If a brother or sister is without clothing and in need of daily food, and one of you says to them, "Go in peace, be warmed and be filled," and yet you do not give them what is necessary for their body, what use is that? Even so faith, if it has no works, is dead, being by itself. (James 2:15–17)

And John says that true love for God goes hand in hand with love for people.

> We know love by this, that He laid down His life for us; and we ought to lay down our lives for the brethren. But whoever has the world's goods, and

beholds his brother in need and closes his heart against him, how does the love of God abide in him? Little children, let us not love with word or with tongue, but in deed and truth. (1 John 3:16–18)

Unfortunately, many of us were taught to avert our eyes and quickly walk by those in need. "Don't get involved," we were told. "Look out for number one." Such advice, however, makes victims of us all, as one man has written:

If I just do my thing and you do yours, we stand in danger of losing each other and ourselves. . . . We are fully ourselves only in relation to each other; the I detached from a Thou disintegrates. I do not find you by chance; I find you by an active life of reaching out.[4]

A caring, compassionate heart is absolutely essential to the message we have to share with the world. As another man has said, "People don't care how much you know until they know how much you care."[5] Others won't hear our words until they see Christ's love demonstrated in our outstretched hands.

 Living Insights

Like the road from Jerusalem to Jericho, the road of life snakes through a landscape of jagged hills and unforeseen dangers. Sometimes we are the victim along the trail, attacked by circumstances that leave us bloodied and helpless. Sometimes we are the priest or the Levite, too busy or maybe too overwhelmed or afraid to stop and help. Sometimes, though, we are the Samaritan, understanding the pain of the victim and reaching out in compassion and love.

Jesus' story touches us all. We've been there. We're there right now.

4. Walter Tubbs, as quoted by Amitai Etzioni in *An Immodest Agenda: Rebuilding America before the Twenty-First Century* (New York, N.Y.: McGraw-Hill Book Co., New Press, 1983), p. 45.

5. Michael LeBoeuf, *How to Win Customers and Keep Them for Life* (New York, N.Y.: G. P. Putnam's Sons, 1987), p. 35.

At this place in your life, with whom can you identify most? The victim, the religious pair, or the Samaritan? Give a reason or two for your choice.

_____

_____

_____

If you feel like the wounded stranger, what is Jesus' story saying to you about receiving help?

_____

_____

_____

If you feel like the priest or Levite, what do you think is blocking you from showing love to the hurting neighbors in your path?

_____

_____

_____

How can you overcome some of these emotional/mental obstacles?

_____

_____

_____

If you feel like the Samaritan, you may want to help all the wounded victims along your path. Bruised and bleeding bodies seem to be strewn everywhere. How do you decide which neighbor to help?

That's a difficult question to answer. Maybe a few of these thoughts will serve as guides:

- I can't help everyone.

- I can help some people more than others.

- Sometimes the most loving thing to do is encourage people to help themselves.

- I have to make wise choices with the limited resources God has given me.

  What guidelines of your own would you add?

  _____

  _____

  _____

  Using these guidelines, can you think of one hurting neighbor to whom you can show kindness?

  _____

  What can you do to express Christ's love to this person? Make a brief plan, and commit yourself to carrying it out.

  _____

  _____

  _____

  _____

Chapter 4

A NONEXCLUSIVE COVENANT

Selected Scriptures

Do you remember thinking about heaven when you were a child? Did you ever hope there would be horses in heaven? Or roller coasters? Or pizza? Author Bill Adler asked some children what they thought about death and heaven. Their responses give us a delightful peek into a child's imagination about the world beyond. Here are a few samples.

> When you die, you don't have to do homework in heaven unless your teacher is there too.
>
> Marsha W., 9

> A good doctor can help you so you won't die. A bad doctor sends you to heaven.
>
> Raymond L., 10

> When you die, they bury you in the ground and your soul goes to heaven, but your body can't go to heaven because it's too crowded up there already.
>
> Jimmy G., 8

> Only the good people go to heaven. The other people go where it's hot all the time like in Florida.
>
> Judy P., 9[1]

We smile at a child's view of heaven. But is our view much better? No human can fully grasp what heaven is like. Its wonders and beauties stretch far beyond our earthly understanding. However, there is one aspect of glory that we can begin to understand: Heaven is a place for people of every race, culture, color, and age.

One of the first verses a child memorizes is,

> "For God so loved the world, that He gave His only begotten Son, that whoever believes in Him should not perish, but have eternal life." (John 3:16)

God loves "the world"—not just people like ourselves. And

---

1. Bill Adler, "You Don't Have to Do Homework in Heaven!" Source unknown.

"whoever" believes in His crucified Son—regardless of nationality—will have eternal life.

Sometimes, though, we think that God is interested only in people who talk and act the way we do. But that's not so. In this chapter, we want to widen our tunnel vision. We want to see the world as God sees it and catch a shining glimpse of the true heaven.

Salvation: A Universal Offer

We already know what earth is like—full of hatred, greed, and sin. Because we have rebelled against God, we live under a sentence of death. In such a state, how can anyone go to heaven? John shows us the way in 1 John 2:1–2, where he lays the foundation for God's redemptive relationship with the world:

> My little children, I am writing these things to you that you may not sin. And if anyone sins, we have an Advocate with the Father, Jesus Christ the righteous; and He Himself is the propitiation for our sins; and not for ours only, but also for those of the whole world.

Moved by love, God offered His Son on the altar of the cross, and Jesus Himself became the *propitiation*—that is, the pleasing sacrifice that satisfied God's wrath against sin.[2] With the barrier of judgment removed, God now opens wide His arms and bids all people to come to Him in faith and be cleansed by the blood of Christ (see 1:7).

As Jesus announced, God's offer of salvation is wonderfully inclusive.

> "And I, if I be lifted up from the earth, will draw all men to Myself." (John 12:32)

The apostle Paul also expressed God's generous heart for the world:

> This is good and acceptable in the sight of God our

2. John R. W. Stott further defines *propitiation*: "It is an appeasement of the wrath of God by the love of God through the gift of God. The initiative is not taken by man, nor even by Christ, but by God Himself in sheer unmerited love." *The Epistles of John*, The Tyndale New Testament Commentaries Series (Grand Rapids, Mich.: William B. Eerdmans Publishing Co., 1964), p. 88.

Savior, who desires all men to be saved and to come to the knowledge of the truth. (1 Tim. 2:3–4)

And so did Peter:

The Lord is not slow about His promise, as some count slowness, but is patient toward you, not wishing for any to perish but for all to come to repentance. (2 Pet. 3:9)

The word *all* chimes in these verses like a liberty bell, ringing out to every nation and every culture. It penetrates racial barriers and crosses ethnic lines. It resounds through the palaces of kings and echoes through the poorest ghettos. In every language and every dialect, God shouts His nonexclusive offer to humankind: Eternal life to all who believe!

Heaven: A Multicultural Scene

To appreciate the full scope of this salvation, we must look beyond earth's divisions and prejudices and study the realities of God's heavenly kingdom. John's vision in the book of Revelation serves as our celestial telescope, giving us a spectacular view of the throne room of God. Keep in mind that these scenes aren't the imaginations of a child or the speculations of a theologian; they are revelations of our glorified Savior given to John by God Himself (see Rev. 1:1).

After these things I looked, and behold, a door standing open in heaven, and the first voice which I had heard, like the sound of a trumpet speaking with me, said, "Come up here, and I will show you what must take place after these things." Immediately I was in the Spirit; and behold, a throne was standing in heaven, and One sitting on the throne. And He who was sitting was like a jasper stone and a sardius in appearance; and there was a rainbow around the throne, like an emerald in appearance. And around the throne were twenty-four thrones; and upon the thrones I saw twenty-four elders sitting, clothed in white garments, and golden crowns on their heads. And from the throne proceed flashes of lightning and sounds and peals of thunder. And

there were seven lamps of fire burning before the
throne, which are the seven Spirits of God; and
before the throne there was, as it were, a sea of glass
like crystal; and in the center and around the throne,
four living creatures full of eyes in front and behind.
(Rev. 4:1–6)

Each of the creatures had six wings, and day and night their
voices thundered through heaven:

"Holy, Holy, Holy, is the Lord God, the Almighty,
who was and who is and who is to come." (v. 8b)

Then John saw the twenty-four elders fall before God, cast their
crowns at His feet in humble worship (v. 10), and cry out,

"Worthy art Thou, our Lord and our God, to receive
glory and honor and power; for Thou didst create
all things, and because of Thy will they existed, and
were created." (v. 11)

As the vision continues in chapter 5, it builds momentum like
a swelling wave.

And I saw in the right hand of Him who sat on
the throne a book written inside and on the back,
sealed up with seven seals. And I saw a strong angel
proclaiming with a loud voice, "Who is worthy to
open the book and to break its seals?" And no one
in heaven, or on the earth, or under the earth, was
able to open the book, or to look into it. And I
began to weep greatly, because no one was found
worthy to open the book, or to look into it. (vv. 1–4)

The book contains the judgments of God with which He will
bring justice to the world. No wonder John weeps. If the seals
remain unbroken, all hope for justice is lost. Is no one worthy to
open the book?

And one of the elders said to me, "Stop weeping;
behold, the Lion that is from the tribe of Judah, the
Root of David, has overcome so as to open the book
and its seven seals." And I saw between the throne
(with the four living creatures) and the elders a
Lamb standing, as if slain, having seven horns and

seven eyes, which are the seven Spirits of God, sent
out into all the earth. (vv. 5–6)

Called "the Lion," yet pictured as a slain lamb that has come
back to life, this figure can be none other than Jesus Christ (see
John 1:29; 1 Pet. 1:19).

And He came, and He took it out of the right hand
of Him who sat on the throne. And when He had
taken the book, the four living creatures and the
twenty-four elders fell down before the Lamb, having each one a harp, and golden bowls full of incense,
which are the prayers of the saints. (Rev. 5:7–8)

The twenty-four elders who earlier offered their praise to God
now bow before the Lamb.

And they sang a new song, saying,
"Worthy art Thou to take the book, and to
break its seals; for Thou wast slain, and didst
purchase for God with Thy blood men from
every tribe and tongue and people and nation.[3] And Thou hast made them to be a
kingdom and priests to our God; and they
will reign upon the earth." (vv. 9–10)

The word *men* was added by the translators to smooth out the
reading. It wasn't in the original text, and perhaps it wasn't meant
to be. Maybe John intended the verse to be incomplete to under-
score Christ's universal appeal. Before Him, all people stand on
level ground—men and women, young and old, rich and poor. As
Paul proclaimed,

There is neither Jew nor Greek, there is neither slave
nor free man, there is neither male nor female; for
you are all one in Christ Jesus. (Gal. 3:28)

During the Olympics, when people from every nation gather in
one stadium, we get a taste of world unity. But nowhere has anyone
seen a crowd like the one we will see in heaven. South African
whites will link arms with South African blacks; Croatians, with

---

3. Is there any significance to the order of the words *tribe, tongue, people,* and *nation*? Probably
not, since they appear in different order in 7:9, 13:7, and 14:6.

Serbs; Arabs, with Jews. With one voice, the redeemed will lift their song in praise of the Savior:

> And I looked, and I heard the voice of many angels around the throne and the living creatures and the elders; and the number of them was myriads of myriads, and thousands of thousands, saying with a loud voice,
> "Worthy is the Lamb that was slain to receive power and riches and wisdom and might and honor and glory and blessing."
> And every created thing which is in heaven and on the earth and under the earth and on the sea, and all things in them, I heard saying,
> "To Him who sits on the throne, and to the Lamb, be blessing and honor and glory and dominion forever and ever." (Rev. 5:11–13)

What a day that will be! The start of unending happiness! However, along with the joy we anticipate, we must remember a sobering realization: Not everyone will be there, for not everyone will receive Christ as Savior. This thought leads us to a couple of very important questions.

You: Some Questions to Consider

First, will you be there? Have you trusted Christ for your salvation? Some people give the excuse that Christianity is a Western religion. "Jesus is for Americans or Europeans," they claim. But our glimpse into heaven proves that Jesus belongs to the world, not just the West. Does He belong to you?

Second, if you are a Christian, do you share Christ's global mind-set? It's easy to settle into a circle of friends who look like us and talk like us and then forget about the world at our doorstep. Without realizing it, we turn our backs on people of other cultures, excluding them from our lives and our Lord. Stepping out of those circles sounds risky at first. But it's the only way the people of the world are going to hear the gospel.

Are you willing to reach across ethnic lines to share Christ's love? It's a great way to bring a little heaven down to earth.

Living Insights

The Berlin Wall had existed for so long it had become part of the landscape. The people were accustomed to it. It had become normal . . . until the day it came down. In November 1989, the wall separating East and West Berlin fell in a heap of dust and debris. For the first time in nearly thirty years, people from two different worlds embraced one another in a display of peace and unity.

Is there is a wall of prejudice or indifference in your heart that needs to come down too? How can we tear down the ethnic barriers we set up and begin to see people as God sees them?

One way is by praying for those in your world who are different from you. Prayer pulls down the walls we build around our homes and our lives. It takes our eyes off our own desires and fills our hearts with concern for others.

Is there a family of another nationality or culture in your neighborhood who doesn't know Christ? Jot down a prayer that they will become a part of God's heavenly community.

_____

_____

_____

You may want to share this prayer with your family or friends and make it a part of your regular mealtime prayers.

What else can you and your family do to share Christ's love for them? It might simply be taking the time to stop and chat. Or you might invite them over for a meal. What ideas do you have?

_____

_____

_____

Having taken this first step, try expanding your global vision by praying for different ethnic communities in your city. Through your church, you may want to target a certain area for evangelism or children's outreaches.

Here are some other ways you can tear down the cultural wall:

- visit a church that is ethnically different from yours
- combine the two churches for an interracial church picnic
- experience another culture by participating in a short-term mission
- read Paul Borthwick's book *How to Be a World-Class Christian* (Wheaton, Ill.: Scripture Press Publications, Victor Books, 1991)

In God's kingdom, there are no walls. No borders divide nation from nation. No language barriers keep people apart. In God's kingdom, we are one.

Chapter 5

STRENGTHENING YOUR GRIP
ON EVANGELISM
Acts 8:26–39

Does sharing your faith rank right up there with root canals on your list of desired activities? Don't feel alone. It seems that most Christians would rather do anything than witness. Why? Well, for several reasons.

One is *ignorance*—we don't really know how to go about it. Another reason is *indifference*. We have other things to think about, and besides, plenty of evangelists out there can do the job better than we could. Third, we're *afraid*. Nobody likes being made a fool of or being asked questions they can't answer—especially by a stranger. And what if the response is hostile? The whole idea is just too intimidating. Also, many of us have an unpleasant memory of a *bad experience* when someone grabbed us by the collar and shoved the gospel down our throat. We remember that embarrassed, intruded-upon, pressured feeling, and the last thing we want to do is make someone else feel that way.

We've probably all been in situations—maybe on a plane, maybe at a convention—when the topic of religion came up and we had to face that inevitable dialogue with a nonbeliever. We've usually ended up feeling awkward and uncomfortable, and we've walked away wondering, What could I have done to not only win a hearing but keep a hearing? How could I have shown Christ to that person in a more understandable way? How could I have kept from sounding so pious or so out of touch with reality?

Good questions. And tucked away in Acts 8 is a series of answers. In this chapter is a story about a man named Philip. He was like most of us, but he was also a fervent evangelist. The principles we find in his life relate to every Christian.

This chapter is also included in the study guide *Strengthening Your Grip*, coauthored by Ken Gire and Gary Matlack, from the Bible-teaching ministry of Charles R. Swindoll (Anaheim, Calif.: Insight for Living, 1995), pp. 107–13.

Philip's Background: From Persecution to Proclamation

In the first century, the seeds of the gospel were scattered by the winds of persecution. With Saul of Tarsus looking on, religious leaders stoned Stephen after his compelling—and convicting—sermon (Acts 7:52–60). Those stones sent ripples of persecution through Jerusalem, driving believers out to all of Judea and Samaria (8:1b). Did persecution dampen their spirits? No, just the opposite:

> Therefore, those who had been scattered went about preaching the word. (v. 4)

One of those scattered, preaching Christians was a man named Philip.

Philip's "Person-to-Person" Experience

Through Philip, God had stirred up the city of Samaria into a state of revival (8:5–13). When the apostles heard that he was up to his ears in new believers, they dispatched Peter and John to help him (vv. 14–25). How encouraging! Their ministry was burgeoning, and people were growing in the love of God. This would be a great place to settle down and nurture new believers, wouldn't it? Well, don't hammer down that tent peg so fast.

Right in the middle of this flourishing metropolitan ministry, the Lord uprooted Philip and set him on a desert road . . . to reach one person. Verses 26–39 record the experience, from which six key words emerge to help us share the gospel with people we encounter.

Sensitivity

> But an angel of the Lord spoke to Philip saying, "Arise and go south to the road that descends from Jerusalem to Gaza." (This is a desert road.) And he arose and went. (vv. 26–27a)

Oh, that we were all so sensitive to God's leading! Philip "arose and went" immediately after the angel directed him southward. No questions. No bargaining. No complaints about being pulled from city revival to wilderness witnessing. He just went.

What about us? Do we keep our spiritual sails unfurled, watching for them to flutter with a gust of God's wind? Or do we prefer to row along at our own speed, oblivious to the breeze? Through

Scripture, circumstances, and inner promptings, the Holy Spirit will guide us. But reaching others for Christ requires that we stay sensitive to His leading, whether we're on a plane, in a classroom, in the office, or sitting in our neighbor's living room.

Availability

> And behold, there was an Ethiopian eunuch, a court official of Candace, queen of the Ethiopians, who was in charge of all her treasure; and he had come to Jerusalem to worship. And he was returning and sitting in his chariot, and was reading the prophet Isaiah. And the Spirit said to Philip, "Go up and join this chariot." (vv. 27b–29)

Availability and sensitivity are twins—with slight variations. Both entail openness to God's leading; but where *sensitivity* emphasizes the ears (listening to and initially responding to God), *availability* focuses more on the feet (moving them in whatever direction God specifies). Sensitivity says, "I hear You, Lord, and I'm on my way." Availability says, "OK, where's the next turn?" Once Philip left Samaria, he kept his eyes open for God's road signs.

The Spirit led him to a royal eunuch poring over the Scriptures in his chariot. Commentator Simon Kistemaker describes this traveler as "the chief treasurer. He has the prominent position of chancellor of the exchequer, or finance minister, in charge of the royal treasury and national revenue" of Ethiopia.[1] William Barclay sheds light on the purpose of the man's journey:

> This eunuch had been to Jerusalem to worship. In those days the world was full of people who were weary of the many gods and the loose morals of the nations. They came to Judaism and there found the one God and the austere moral standards which gave life meaning. If they accepted Judaism and were circumcised they were called *proselytes*; if they did not go that length but continued to attend the Jewish synagogues and to read the Jewish scriptures they were called *God-fearers*. This Ethiopian must have

1. Simon J. Kistemaker, *New Testament Commentary: Exposition of the Acts of the Apostles* (Grand Rapids, Mich.: Baker Book House, 1990), p. 312.

been one of these searchers who came to rest in Judaism either as a proselyte or a God-fearer.[2]

So Philip, taking his directions from the Spirit of God, pulled up beside this inquisitive official.

Initiative

As he approached the chariot, Philip heard the familiar words of Isaiah 53 read contemplatively by the Ethiopian. What do you think was going through the evangelist's mind just then? "Oh, this is too good to be true—he's reading about the Messiah. OK, deep breaths, deep breaths. I've got him now. Just another minute and . . ." Not likely, judging from the text:

> And when Philip had run up, he heard him reading Isaiah the prophet, and said, "Do you understand what you are reading?" (v. 30)

Philip started with a simple, yet thoughtful, question—and waited for an answer. He took the initiative in the conversation, setting a tone that didn't try to impress or insult. He just asked a question. There's nothing like a good question to open people up and introduce the topic of spirituality. You might want to try some of these:

- "What do you think is wrong with the world today?"

- "Who do you think is the greatest person who ever lived?"

- "You know, there's a lot about the 'religious right' in the news today. I'm curious, what's your perception of Christianity?"

- "Do you find in your line of work that most people are honest and treat others fairly?"

Just remember, taking the initiative doesn't mean we have to bully people with our message. Truth and tact can come bundled in the same package.

Tactfulness

The gospel of Christ isn't a box of sweets. Not everyone who gets

---

2. William Barclay, *The Acts of the Apostles*, rev. ed., The Daily Study Bible Series (Philadelphia, Pa.: Westminster Press, 1976), pp. 68–69.

a taste will say, "What a treat. Can I have some more?" The message will offend many, simply because it makes clear distinctions between right and wrong (see Matt. 15:12; Rom. 9:33). We, however, don't have to add to the offense by *being offensive*. In fact, one of the most important principles we can remember is to *put ourselves in the other person's shoes*. If you remember nothing else, remember that. The Cross is to be offensive, not Christians (see 1 Cor. 1:18–25).

Philip treated the eunuch with respect, courtesy, and dignity. In answer to Philip's question, the eunuch responded:

> "Well, how could I, unless someone guides me?"
> And he invited Philip to come up and sit with him.
> Now the passage of Scripture which he was reading was this:
> "He was led as a sheep to slaughter;
> And as a lamb before its shearer is silent,
> So He does not open His mouth.
> In humiliation His judgment was taken
>   away;
> Who shall relate His generation?
> For His life is removed from the earth."
> And the eunuch answered Philip and said, "Please tell me, of whom does the prophet say this? Of himself, or of someone else?" (Acts 8:31–34)

Philip asked a question (v. 30) and waited for an answer. He listened. He was attentive. He waited to be invited into the chariot. And he lovingly led the eunuch through the pages of the Old Testament to Christ Himself (v. 35).

Our attitude and actions make a big difference in whether we're granted a hearing. Ironically, some Christians seem most un-Christlike when they're sharing His very words. We need to dispense with pushiness and pride and instead demonstrate Jesus' kindness and humility. Listen more. Judge less. Talk *with* people, not *at* them. Smile. Look the person in the eye. Offer a firm handshake.

By the way, there's nothing winsome about bad breath or body odor. The difference between repelling and attracting a non-Christian could be as simple as a breath mint or stick of deodorant.

Isn't it worth the effort to be tactful, courteous, and pleasant— considering how precious this unsaved person is to God?

Precision

Philip was not only courteous, he was also precise. That is, he kept the conversation focused on Christ.

> And Philip opened his mouth, and beginning from this Scripture he preached Jesus to him. (v. 35)

We think of preaching as speaking before a large crowd. Philip, however, "preached" to one person. Did he stand up, then, in the chariot and ask for a show of hands or deliver an altar call? No. The word for *preached* here can be translated simply "told him the good news" (NIV).

Starting with the eunuch's frame of reference, Isaiah 53, Philip shared the good news of Jesus Christ. He didn't debate various theories on when the book of Isaiah was written. He avoided bad-mouthing the synagogue for failing to declare Christ. He didn't present a survey of world religions. Nor did he condemn the eunuch for his employment in a pagan government. He simply shared Christ.

When we engage others in this kind of conversation, we need to understand that many are in the midst of inner distractions. Some may have been mistreated by Christians. Others are running from God, sending up smoke screens to avoid facing their predicament. Still others are downright antagonistic toward the faith. When such dynamics enter our discussions with nonbelievers, we must acknowledge their concerns but keep the spotlight on the death and resurrection of Jesus Christ.

Decisiveness

> And as they went along the road they came to some water; and the eunuch said, "Look! Water! What prevents me from being baptized?" And Philip said, "If you believe with all your heart, you may." And he answered and said, "I believe that Jesus Christ is the Son of God." And he ordered the chariot to stop; and they both went down into the water, Philip as well as the eunuch; and he baptized him. (Acts 8:36–38)

"Can I be baptized now?"

"Wait a minute," said Philip. "Do you believe what I've shared with you?"

Having presented the message, Philip helped the eunuch understand that following Christ involves making a clear decision.

37

A word of caution here. Some evangelism techniques emphasize "closing the sale." In other words, guiding people to the point of decision, getting them to pray the "sinner's prayer" before we leave them. But there are a couple of dangers in this kind of approach.

If we make a "prayer of salvation" our goal, we might be tempted to manipulate the message to that end—making the gospel something it's not. Such an approach can also cause us to stop viewing the lost as real people with real needs. Instead, they become "targets," potential notches on our Bible.

We need to realize that our responsibility is to clearly communicate the message, not convert sinners. It is the Holy Spirit who draws people to Christ and provides the gift of eternal life.

When God does lead individuals to embrace the gospel during a conversation, as He did with the eunuch, we can help them understand their decision and get them started on the road to new life. Which is what Philip did. And the eunuch "went on his way rejoicing" (v. 39b), carrying the seeds of the gospel home to Africa.

Closing Comments

Many evangelism-shy Christians say to themselves, "I can be a silent partner in winning the world to Christ. I'll simply live my faith instead of talking about it all the time."

It's true—when it comes to witnessing, few things are as important as living a godly life. But to say that's all it takes is like saying a plane needs only one wing to fly. As Paul observed,

> But how shall they ask [the Lord] to save them unless they believe in him? And how can they believe in him if they have never heard about him? And how can they hear about him unless someone tells them? (Rom. 10:14 LB)

God has placed you where He has placed no one else. No one else in the world has the same relationships you have. No one will stand in the same grocery store line at exactly the same moment you do. No one else will come across a hungering diplomat in the desert at exactly the same time you do.

God hasn't put you in those places merely to model the truth. Listen for the voice of the Spirit to whisper in your ear. Watch for the stranger on the road. And be aware of your opportunities to go where He would send you.

Living Insights

John Kramp begins his book on evangelism, *Out of Their Faces and into Their Shoes*, with this honest observation:

> Christians and non-Christians agree on one thing— both dislike evangelism. The word alone conjures up images of "in your face" confrontation. Therefore Christians usually avoid gospel showdowns and most non-Christians are relieved they do.[3]

Is your head nodding in agreement with his statement? Have you ever been part of a "gospel showdown" with a non-Christian? If so, how did you feel afterward? How do you think the other person felt?

_____

_____

_____

Kramp continues,

> When evangelism is attempted it rarely begins with *"in your shoes"* empathy. If Christians really understood the spiritually lost people around them, they would talk about faith more naturally. Evangelism would be more of a conversation and less of a high-pressure sales pitch.[4]

Empathy shows respect for the other person's opinions and feelings. It says, "I care." It builds a bridge of acceptance and understanding. How did Philip's simple question, "Do you understand what you are reading?" show empathy toward the eunuch?

_____

_____

_____

3 . John Kramp, *Out of Their Faces and into Their Shoes* (Nashville, Tenn.: Broadman and Holman Publishers, 1995), p. 1.

4. Kramp, *Out of Their Faces and into Their Shoes*, p. 1.

What attitude or perspective do you think is required to step into a lost person's shoes?

_____

_____

_____

What are some ways you can show empathy toward a lost friend of yours?

_____

_____

_____

The first part of *Out of Their Faces and into Their Shoes* is titled "You Can Learn a Lot by Getting Lost." Every once in a while, try getting lost—that is, try to feel what it is like to be a non-Christian, separated from God. The view from that side of the fence is bound to open your eyes, as well as soften your heart.

Chapter 6

"MR. SMITH, MEET YOUR SUBSTITUTE"

Selected Scriptures

S everal years ago, a certain auto manufacturer launched an unusual ad campaign. The commercials featured a lush meadow, a flock of birds fluttering into the sky, a glistening stream trickling through the forest. But they never showed the car! Only the name, "Infiniti," appeared at the end. The purpose was to create a positive feeling about the car; but after a while, the ads lost their appeal. People wanted to see the product, not just the marketing strategy.

In the same way, if we're not careful, our efforts at evangelism can become just as hollow. We can create a positive feeling for the unsaved in our churches. We can utilize eye-catching, state-of-the-art modes of communication. We can even reach across cultural boundaries with genuine gestures of love. But if we don't reveal the gospel—or if our gospel message comes across obscure or hesitant—we haven't connected where it's most important.

Do you have a clear picture of the gospel? Have you ever felt frustrated trying to put what you know into words? In this chapter, we'll show you one approach to explaining the true meaning of the Cross to a non-Christian.

Four Major Issues

Meet Mr. Smith. Like many spiritually lost people, he is vaguely aware of God, but he doesn't really know who He is or how to find Him. Mr. Smith could be our neighbor, coworker, or friend. Our job is simply to introduce him to the Savior who loves him. But what do we say? Where do we begin?

Our Condition: Totally Depraved

The first truth Mr. Smith must grasp is rather personal. One look in the mirror of Scripture, and the human condition becomes painfully clear:

> As it is written,
> > "There is none righteous, not even one;

41

There is none who understands,
There is none who seeks for God;
All have turned aside, together they have
    become useless;
There is none who does good,
There is not even one." (Rom. 3:10–12)

We are sinners through and through—totally depraved. Now that doesn't mean we've committed every atrocity known to humankind. We're not as *bad* as we can be, just as *bad off* as we can be. If depravity were blue, we'd be blue all over. Sin colors all our thoughts, motives, words, and actions.

Everything around us bears the smudge marks of our sinful nature. Despite our best efforts to create a perfect world, crime statistics continue to soar, divorce rates keep climbing, and families keep crumbling. Some people tell us not to worry, to put our faith in technology and human ingenuity. Yet even here our creativity has outpaced our morality.

Something has gone terribly wrong in our society and in ourselves, something deadly. For, contrary to how the world would repackage it, sin does not equal rugged individuality and freedom; it equals death. Just take a look at depravity's "benefits":

> And just as they did not see fit to acknowledge God any longer, God gave them over to a depraved mind, to do those things which are not proper, being filled with all unrighteousness, wickedness, greed, evil; full of envy, murder, strife, deceit, malice; they are gossips, slanderers, haters of God, insolent, arrogant, boastful, inventors of evil, disobedient to parents, without understanding, untrustworthy, unloving, unmerciful. (1:28–31)

As Paul says later in Romans, "The wages of sin is death" (6:23)—our emotional and physical death through sin's destructiveness, and our spiritual death from God's righteous judgment of our sin.

God's Character: Infinitely Holy

Our very awareness that things are not as they should be points to a standard of goodness beyond ourselves. That standard is God Himself. And God's standard of holiness contrasts starkly to our sinful condition.

Scripture says that "God is light, and in Him there is no darkness at all" (1 John 1:5). He is absolutely righteous—which creates a problem for us. If He is so pure, how can we who are so impure relate to Him? How can we who live in darkness endure the scrutiny of His blinding light? How can we hope to escape the sentence of death for our sins?

Perhaps we could try being better people, try to tilt the balance in favor of our good deeds. Throughout history, people have attempted to live up to God's standard by keeping His law. Unfortunately, no one can come close to satisfying the law's demands. J. B. Phillips' translation of Romans 3 states:

> No man can justify himself before God by a perfect performance of the Law's demands—indeed it is the straight-edge of the Law that shows us how crooked we are.
> . . . For there is no distinction to be made anywhere: everyone has sinned, everyone falls short of the beauty of God's plan. (vv. 20, 22b–23 PHILLIPS)

So here we are, sinners by nature, sinners by choice, trying to pull ourselves up by our bootstraps and attain a relationship with our holy Creator. But every time, we fall flat on our faces. We can't live a good enough life to make up for our sin, because God's standard isn't "good enough"—it's perfection. And we can't make amends for the offense our sin has created without dying for it.

What can get us out of this mess?

Our Need: A Substitute

If someone could live perfectly, honoring God's law, and would bear sin's death penalty for us, then we would be saved from our predicament. But is there such a person? Thankfully, yes!

Mr. Smith, meet your substitute: Jesus Christ.

> [God] made [Jesus Christ] who knew no sin to be sin on our behalf, that we might become the righteousness of God in Him. (2 Cor. 5:21)

God's Provision: A Savior

God rescued us by sending His Son, Jesus, to die for our sins on the cross (see 1 John 4:9–10). Jesus was fully human and fully divine, a truth that ensures His understanding of our weaknesses,

His power to forgive, and His ability to bridge the gap between God and us. Jesus' substitutionary death reconciles us to God, as Paul explains in Romans 5:

> For while we were still helpless, at the right time Christ died for the ungodly. For one will hardly die for a righteous man; though perhaps for the good man someone would dare even to die. But God demonstrates His own love toward us, in that while we were yet sinners, Christ died for us. Much more then, having now been justified by His blood, we shall be saved from the wrath of God through Him. For if while we were enemies, we were reconciled to God through the death of His Son, much more, having been reconciled, we shall be saved by His life. And not only this, but we also exult in God through our Lord Jesus Christ, through whom we have now received the reconciliation. (vv. 6–11)

Or in short form, we are "justified as a gift by His grace through the redemption which is in Christ Jesus" (3:24). Two words in this verse bear further explanation: *justified* and *redemption*.

Justification is God's act of mercy, in which He declares believing sinners righteous, while they are still in their sinning state. Justification doesn't mean "just as if we'd never sinned," because God knows we've sinned and declares us righteous anyway. Neither does it mean that God *makes* us righteous, so that we never sin again. Because Jesus took our sin upon Himself and suffered our judgment, God forgives our debt and proclaims us PARDONED.

Redemption is God's act of paying the ransom price to release us from our bondage to sin. Held hostage by Satan, we were shackled by the iron chains of sin and death. Like any loving parent whose child has been kidnapped, God willingly paid the ransom. And what a price He paid! He gave His only Son to bear all the sins of humankind—past, present, and future. Jesus' death and resurrection broke our chains and set us free to become children of God (see Rom. 6:16–18, 22; Gal. 4:4–7).

Three Crucial Questions

Three questions may emerge in Mr. Smith's mind that we need to answer. The first is this: *"Is there any hope for lost sinners?"* Yes—

Christ! We tend to add to the formula. However, we are not saved by Christ *and* the church, by Christ *and* water baptism, by Christ *and* sincerity, or by Christ *and* morality. Christ alone saves us (see John 14:6; Acts 4:12).

Another question is, *"Isn't there any work for a seeker to do?"* No—just believe! Salvation is "a gift by His grace" (Rom. 3:24). We simply receive the benefits of what Christ has done for us. If we earned even a sliver of our salvation, we'd have something to boast about. But, since Christ did all the work, Paul concludes,

> Where then is boasting? It is excluded. By what kind of law? Of works? No, but by a law of faith. For we maintain that a man is justified by faith apart from works of the Law. (vv. 27–28)

Later he argues:

> For what does the Scripture say? "And Abraham believed God, and it was reckoned to him as righteousness." Now to the one who works, his wage is not reckoned as a favor, but as what is due. (4:3–4)

Salvation is a gift, not a wage. On payday, your boss hands you a check. You earned it. Your boss owes it to you. You take the credit for it. But suppose your boss attaches a bonus of a thousand dollars, in spite of your poor performance that month. Now that would be a gift of grace (and a miracle too!).

Can you imagine how God feels when we try to pay for the gift of salvation He bought for us? It's like going to a friend's house for a delicious meal, then pulling out your wallet and asking, "OK, what do I owe you for dinner?" The meal is free, and so is our salvation. Enjoy!

Third, *"Is there any way to lose the gift of salvation?"* No—never! If our salvation depended on us to obtain it, then it would depend on us to keep it. But, since it is a gift, it's ours to hold and treasure.

> Salvation is simply a gift. It's simple, but it wasn't easy. It's free, but it wasn't cheap. It's yours, but it isn't automatic. You must receive it. When you do, it is yours forever.[1]

---

1. Charles R. Swindoll, *Growing Deep in the Christian Life: Essential Truths for Becoming Strong in the Faith* (Grand Rapids, Mich.: Zondervan Publishing House, 1995), p. 242.

Two Possible Responses

Mr. Smith has two choices: he can either believe in Christ and accept the gift of salvation, or he can not believe and reject the gift.

Now, if he rejects Christ, God won't swell with rage and zap him with a lightning bolt. He won't retaliate by making his car break down or his boss fire him. God never twists our arm to take His gift of salvation.

One Final Reminder

But there is one final factor—we don't have forever to make our decision. Sin is a terminal disease. When the moment of death overtakes us, our choice to accept or reject Christ is set for eternity (Heb. 9:27).

We can offer a cup of cool water to someone dying of thirst, but we can't make that person drink; in the same sense, we can introduce Mr. Smith to the Savior, but we can't make him trust Him. Ultimately, the decision is his.

 Living Insights

One of the best tools you can use in explaining the gospel is a simple diagram. You can sketch it anywhere—on a napkin at a restaurant, in the sand at the beach, on the back of a business card. The following illustration is based on the four crucial issues of the gospel we covered in the lesson. Take a few moments to study it; and make sure to look up the verses and slip them into your memory.

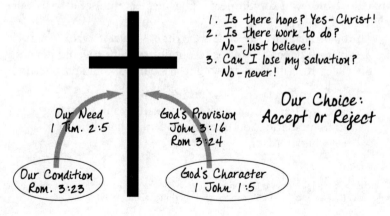

1. Is there hope? Yes - Christ!
2. Is there work to do? No - just believe!
3. Can I lose my salvation? No - never!

Our Choice: Accept or Reject

Our Need
1 Tim. 2:5

God's Provision
John 3:16
Rom 3:24

Our Condition
Rom. 3:23

God's Character
1 John 1:5

Do you think you can talk your way through this diagram? Try following this procedure:

1. On a separate piece of paper, begin by sketching the circle on the left and writing "Our Condition, Romans 3:23." Review the section in the lesson on this point, and put it in your own words.

2. Draw the other circle, and write "God's Character, 1 John 1:5." Review this section, and try restating it. To help the person visualize the barrier between us and God, draw the vertical line of the cross between the two circles.

3. Sketch the arrow that goes from left to right, and write "Our Need, 1 Timothy 2:5." Explain this point from the lesson.

4. Finally, pencil in the arrow that goes from right to left, and finish the cross by drawing the horizontal line. Write "God's Provision, John 3:16; Romans 3:24." Review this point from the lesson.

After you finish explaining what Christ has accomplished for us on the Cross, write down the three questions, answering them one at a time. Conclude by writing "Our Choice: Accept or Reject." Your purpose here is not to manipulate a decision but simply to lay out the fact that the gospel requires a response. Either we believe it or we don't.

Some people may not be ready to accept Christ, yet they may not be willing to reject Him either. God never forces His grace on anyone, and neither should we. However, we can help the person see that not accepting is really the same as rejecting. There is no middle ground.

If the person needs time to think, we should give them plenty of room. Before concluding, we may ask them if they can pinpoint what issue or question is holding them back. Sometimes talking about it will help them resolve it. You may also wish to put into their hands one of these books: *Who Is This Jesus?* by Michael Green (Nashville, Tenn.: Thomas Nelson Publishers, Oliver Nelson, 1992); or *Reason to Believe: A Response to Common Objections to Christianity* by R. C. Sproul (Grand Rapids, Mich.: Zondervan Publishing House, 1978).

If the person is ready to accept Christ, that's wonderful! You may encourage your friend to express his or her decision to the Lord in a prayer. There's no magic formula to this prayer. The thief on the cross simply cried out, "Jesus, remember me when You come in Your kingdom!" (Luke 23:42). If your friend needs help, try using the following prayer as a guide:

Dear God,
   I know that my sin has put a barrier between You and me. Thank You for sending Jesus to die in my place. I accept Your gift of eternal life and ask Jesus to be my personal Savior. Please begin to guide my life. Thank You. In Jesus' name, amen.

Never underestimate the power of the gospel. It can change a person's life—forever.

Chapter 7

No Repentance— No Revival

Selected Scriptures

Mention this evangelist in almost any group, and people immediately recognize his name. Loved and admired around the world, he has "preached to more people face to face than anyone else in the history of Christianity."[1] In 1996, he and his wife received the Congressional Gold Medal, the highest civilian honor. The evangelist? Billy Graham.

Since his first crusade, in a small Baptist church in 1939, Billy Graham has been known for his unimpeachable character and unwavering message—a message he best summed up in a news conference before the 1954 Harringay crusade in London:

> I am going to present a God who matters, and who makes claims on the human race. He is a God of love, grace, and mercy, but also a God of judgment. When we break His moral laws, we suffer; when we keep them, we have inward peace and joy. . . . I am calling for a revival that will cause men and women to return to their offices and shops to live out the teaching of Christ in their daily relationships. I am going to preach a Gospel not of despair but of hope—hope for the individual, for society, and for the world.[2]

"I am calling for a revival," he proclaimed in his distinctive North Carolinian drawl. With equal earnestness, we need to call for a revival too—one that begins with us.

Before revival can sweep across our land, it must first blaze within our hearts. We must purify our love for Christ and trim the wicks of our devotion. Only then can His light burn brightly and cleanly in our lives. Only then can those stumbling through the darkness see the true, undiminished glory of the gospel.

1. Sterling W. Huston, *Crusade Evangelism and the Local Church* (Minneapolis, Minn.: World Wide Publications, 1984), p. 24.

2. Billy Graham, as quoted by Huston in *Crusade Evangelism*, p. 22–23.

Significant Turning Points in Days Past

Thousands of years ago, the psalmist fervently prayed for revival:

> Restore us, O God of our salvation,
> And cause Thine indignation toward us to cease.
> Wilt Thou be angry with us forever?
> Wilt Thou prolong Thine anger to all generations?
> Wilt Thou not Thyself revive us again,
> That Thy people may rejoice in Thee? (Ps. 85:4–6)

"Revive us again." Throughout history, God has answered that prayer. In the days of the judges, He chose people like Deborah, Gideon, and Samson. Imperfect people, to be sure, but powerful leaders God used to awaken Israel's spiritual passions and break her bondage to sin. During the kingdom era, revivals were sometimes launched by kings like Hezekiah and Josiah or by prophets like Jeremiah and Jonah, who called for the people to turn from their wickedness and come to God.

After the voices of the Old Testament prophets faded away, a new voice rang out of the desert: "Repent, for the kingdom of heaven is at hand" (Matt. 3:2). It was John the Baptizer, the fore-runner of Christ.

Picking up the torch of John's message of repentance, Jesus showed the world the way to a new spiritual relationship with God (see 4:17). Then, after His death and resurrection, the Spirit-filled apostles fanned out with that same proclamation, setting spiritual fires across the globe. Marching in their footsteps were the reformers—Wycliffe, Luther, Calvin, Savonarola, and Knox, to name a few—each of them sparking revivals in their generations.

The history of revival unfolds like a patchwork quilt, each section displaying a unique work of God in the hearts of people. Holding the pieces together is the crimson thread of repentance. Let's examine this theme more closely, for without repentance there can be no revival.

Biblical Examination of Repentance

Let's plot our course with three questions: What is repentance? Who does it? And why is it important?

What Is Repentance?

The Greek word for repentance, *metanoia*, means "to change

one's thinking, to turn about."[3] It's the idea of a person walking one direction and then turning to head a different way. It involves a change of mind and actions (see Acts 26:19–20, especially the last part of v. 20).

People commonly associate sorrow with repentance. But merely dousing our sins in tears doesn't mean we have repented. An abusive husband may tell his wife he wants to change; he may even weep with sorrow. But until his behavior turns around, he has not fully repented.

John Stott explains the fullness of repentance in his book *Basic Christianity*.

> Repentance is a definite turn from every thought, word, deed and habit which is known to be wrong. It is not sufficient to feel pangs of remorse or to make some kind of apology to God. Fundamentally, repentance is a matter neither of emotion nor of speech. It is an inward change of mind and attitude towards sin which leads to a change of behavior. . . .
>
> Sometimes, true repentance has to include "restitution." This means putting things right with other people, whom we may have injured. All our sins wound God, and nothing we do can heal the wound. Only the atoning death of our Savior, Jesus Christ, can do this. But when our sins have damaged other people, we can sometimes help to repair the damage, and where we can, we must. . . . There may be money or time for us to pay back, rumors to be contradicted, property to return, apologies to be made, or broken relationships to be mended.
>
> We must not be excessively over-scrupulous in this matter, however. It would be foolish to rummage through past years and make an issue of insignificant words or deeds long ago forgotten by the offended person. Nevertheless, we must be realistic about this duty. I have known a student rightly confess to the

---

3. Fritz Rienecker, *A Linguistic Key to the Greek New Testament*, translated and edited by Cleon L. Rogers, Jr. (Grand Rapids, Mich.: Zondervan Publishing House, Regency Reference Library, 1980), p. 6.

university authorities that she had cheated in an exam, and another return text-books which he had lifted from a shop. An army officer sent to the War Department a list of items he had "scrounged." If we really repent, we shall want to do everything in our power to redress the past. We cannot continue to enjoy the fruits of the sins we want to be forgiven.[4]

In his second letter to the Corinthians, Paul rejoices in his readers' sorrow, not because he delights in their sadness, but because their sorrow has blossomed into changed lives.

I now rejoice, not that you were made sorrowful, but that you were made sorrowful to the point of repentance; for you were made sorrowful according to the will of God, in order that you might not suffer loss in anything through us. For the sorrow that is according to the will of God produces a repentance without regret, leading to salvation; but the sorrow of the world produces death. For behold what earnestness this very thing, this godly sorrow, has produced in you: what vindication of yourselves, what indignation, what fear, what longing, what zeal, what avenging of wrong! (2 Cor. 7:9–11a)

Encompassing more than our intellect, more than our emotions, repentance is a whole-life transformation, as Chuck Colson concludes in his book Loving God:

Thus, repentance is replete with radical implications, for a fundamental change of mind not only turns us from the sinful past, but transforms our life plan, values, ethics, and actions as we begin to see the world through God's eyes rather than ours. That kind of transformation requires the ultimate surrender of self.[5]

4. John R. W. Stott, Basic Christianity, 2d ed., rev. (1971; reprint, Grand Rapids, Mich.: William B. Eerdmans, 1989), pp. 110–11.

5. Charles W. Colson, Loving God (Grand Rapids, Mich.: Zondervan Publishing House, 1987), p. 94.

Who Does It?

Are just the unsaved called to the altar of repentance? No, Christ bids the saved to kneel there as well. In Jesus' final message to the church through the apostle John, He called five of the seven churches in Asia Minor to repent (see Rev. 2:5, 16, 21–22; 3:3, 19). From Matthew to Revelation, the theme of repentance forms the front and back covers for the gospel message. It's obvious that it is important to our lives, but why?

Why Is It Important?

First, repentance affirms our allegiance to God. Every time we change our direction and go God's way, we add one more stone to the foundation of our devotion to Him. Second, it demonstrates our commitment to holiness. And third, it releases us from our bondage to sin.

Is it possible for a Christian to be bound by sin? You bet. Satan may not claim us for eternity, but if we let him, he certainly can wrap chains of sin around us in the present. However, the Holy Spirit will speak softly to our hearts when we talk angrily to a friend or deal dishonestly with a coworker. His little warning signals keep us alert to our need for repentance.

What is the Holy Spirit telling you right now? Perhaps you don't need to hear a call to revival as much as a call to repentance— to seriously investigate your attitudes, your tongue, your eyes, your home, your work, your recreation, and your relationships. Are you forging chains of sin in any of those areas? Are they dragging you down and hurting your family and the family of God?

What can you do? A brief but powerful story in the book of Luke lights the way to repentance.

Specific Case Study of One Who Repented

As Jesus was passing through Jericho on His final journey to Jerusalem and the cross,

> behold, there was a man called by the name of Zaccheus; and he was a chief tax-gatherer, and he was rich. And he was trying to see who Jesus was, and he was unable because of the crowd, for he was small in stature. (Luke 19:2–3)

Tax collectors were especially despised in Jesus' day. Donald A.

Hagner explains why.

> (1) They collected money for the foreign power [Rome] that occupied the land of Israel, thus indirectly giving support to this outrage; (2) they were notoriously unscrupulous, growing wealthy at the expense of others of their own people; and (3) their work involved them in regular contact with Gentiles, rendering them ritually unclean. . . . Tax collectors were universally regarded as no better than robbers or thieves.[6]

As chief tax-collector, Zaccheus had accumulated a mountain of wealth, most of it gleaned from the fruit of other men's labor. Yet none of that money was giving him a leg up today. The little man craned his neck. He stood on tiptoe. He wedged an elbow between bodies. But the wall of people, like the religion of his day, remained firm and unforgiving. Still, he had to see this One they called "a friend of tax-gatherers and sinners" (Luke 7:34).

> And he ran on ahead and climbed up into a sycamore tree in order to see Him, for He was about to pass through that way. And when Jesus came to the place, He looked up and said to him, "Zaccheus, hurry and come down, for today I must stay at your house." (19:4–5)

The shock of Jesus' statement must have almost knocked Zaccheus out of the tree. *Stay at my house?* There were probably many things at his house he wouldn't want an esteemed rabbi like Jesus to see. But with one look into the Savior's eyes of love, Zaccheus felt his resistance quickly melt away. "And he hurried and came down, and received Him gladly" (v. 6).

The grace that warmed Zaccheus, however, grated against Jericho's social elite. Verses 7–8 contrast their reaction to Christ with Zaccheus' response:

> And when they saw it, they all began to grumble, saying, "He has gone to be the guest of a man who

6. Donald A. Hagner, "Tax Collector," in *The International Standard Bible Encyclopedia*, gen. ed. Geoffrey W. Bromiley, rev. ed. (Grand Rapids, Mich.: William B. Eerdmans Publishing Co., 1988), vol. 4, p. 742.

is a sinner." And Zaccheus stopped and said to the Lord, "Behold, Lord, half of my possessions I will give to the poor, and if I have defrauded anyone of anything, I will give back four times as much."

Now that is repentance! That's going way beyond the requirements of the Law (see Exod. 22:4; Lev. 6:1–5). With a turn of the wheel, Zaccheus had changed his course 180 degrees. He was a new man. The old Zaccheus had delighted in ripping off the poor and standing above the Law; the new Zaccheus now bubbled over with mercy for the poor and a desire to make things right.

What could change a person so radically? Certainly it wasn't the angry voice of a condemning preacher. No, Jesus wooed him into repentance by accepting him as he was and meeting his human need for dignity, purpose, and love.

Personal Involvement Today

Zaccheus' story shows us that the Lord notices our tiny steps of faith—weak though they may be. Seeing us trembling in the sycamore tree, He extends His hand of mercy and waits for us to receive Him into our lives. Once inside, He quenches our thirsty souls with His grace and love, which naturally overflows in repentance and change.

You may say, "I don't have the strength to change. I've tried, and I can't." But remember, Zaccheus changed after he came to Christ. First he tasted the goodness of the Lord; then he repented. We don't have to scrub ourselves clean before we come to Jesus. He welcomes us as we are, soiled with sin.

Zaccheus gathered just enough faith to climb a sycamore tree, and that may be all the faith you can muster . . . but it is enough. It is the first step toward repentance, the first step to revival.

 Living Insights

Charles Spurgeon once said, "A Christian must never leave off repenting, for I fear he never leaves off sinning."[7]

In the next few moments, you may wish to start the process of

---

7. Charles Haddon Spurgeon, *Spurgeon at His Best,* comp. Tom Carter (Grand Rapids, Mich.: Baker Book House, 1988), p. 174.

repentance, which may begin with a simple prayer like this:

> *Lord, on the outside, everything is fine. I've worked hard to build an appearance of success. My gold rings and silk garments show the world that I'm someone to be admired. But like Zaccheus, I can't look in a mirror without seeing my deficiencies. I can dress them up as much as I want, even in the garb of religion, but my sins and weaknesses still haunt me. What can I do? Is there hope? Can You love a person like me?*

Take some time to honestly open your heart before God now. Then come back and consider the following questions.

Reread Luke 19:1–10. What do you notice about how Jesus related to Zaccheus in the story?

_____

_____

Can you see Jesus showing that same love and acceptance to you?

_____

_____

In what areas of your life do you need to respond to Christ's grace with repentance and change?

_____

_____

What specific actions do you need to take to set things right?

_____

_____

When Christ touches your life with His grace, you won't have to worry about your witness. People will notice Him shining through your countenance. The brightest testimony for Christ is a changed life.

Chapter 8

NO COMPASSION – NO HARVEST

Matthew 9:27–10:5

How do you share your faith? It seems like there are as many methods as there are Christians, doesn't it? But not all hit the target. Some, in fact, are about as effective as shooting ourselves in the foot!

Take the "Eager Beaver Approach," for instance. Christians who use this method blurt out the gospel insensitively to anybody and everybody, regardless of the situation. They care less about the person than about coercing him or her into saying the right words. Aggressively decision-focused, people who use this approach merely want to add another notch to their Bible. This approach is too pushy.

The "Ivy League Approach," which is just the opposite from above, confines itself to reason and intellect. "Let's discuss world religions," this philosophical witness may say, never getting to the heart of the gospel. Although open and respectful, this method rarely mentions sin or our need for God's forgiveness. It's too vague.

Then there's the "Guilt Approach," which flogs people with shame until they crawl to God for mercy. Spewing fire and brimstone, this method plays on people's fears and depicts God as an uncaring, angry judge. It's too manipulative.

Finally, the "Mute Approach" involves being a silent witness for God. People who use this method could be called mime Christians—"No words, please; just look at my life." They may live the gospel, but they don't explain it. This method is too lopsided.

So what's the best method to use? We could make a case for any number of them—lifestyle, open-air, crusade evangelism. We don't have to limit ourselves to only one. We can share Christ on a street corner or in our living room, in a large arena or at someone's front door. Whatever our method, however, we must include certain essentials that God will use to open the door of people's hearts.

Where will we find these essentials? We can uncover them in several scenes from Jesus' life.

Several Scenes in Jesus' Life

Let's join Jesus at a particularly busy time in His three-year ministry.

His notoriety as a teacher and healer has quickly spread to all the villages, and now He can't go anywhere without stirring up a dust cloud of excitement. Anchoring Himself to His mission, though, Jesus refuses to get carried along by the winds of fame. In Matthew 9:1–8, He heals a paralytic, but not before teaching a vital lesson about His authority to forgive sins. In verses 9–17, He shows grace to tax collectors and sinners, modeling for us His "new wine" ministry that bursts the "old wineskins" of tradition. And in verses 18–26, He highlights the power of faith as He heals a woman afflicted with a twelve-year, chronic bleeding problem and resurrects a synagogue official's daughter.

People's reactions to Him run the gamut of emotions. Some people, like the two blind men He encounters next, overflow with a faith that can't be silenced.

> And as Jesus passed on from there, two blind men followed Him, crying out, and saying, "Have mercy on us, Son of David!" And after He had come into the house, the blind men came up to Him, and Jesus said to them, "Do you believe that I am able to do this?" They said to Him, "Yes, Lord." Then He touched their eyes, saying, "Be it done to you according to your faith." And their eyes were opened. And Jesus sternly warned them, saying, "See here, let no one know about this!" But they went out, and spread the news about Him in all that land. (vv. 27–31)

Not everyone, however, is as enamored with Jesus as the blind men are.

> And as they were going out, behold, a dumb man, demon-possessed, was brought to Him. And after the demon was cast out, the dumb man spoke; and the multitudes marveled, saying, "Nothing like this was ever seen in Israel." But the Pharisees were saying, "He casts out the demons by the ruler of the demons." (vv. 32–34)

Jesus either enraptured people or enraged them. He either

sparked reverential awe or inflamed blasphemous anger. No one could stand in His presence and walk away unmoved.

So far we have seen how people responded to Jesus, but have you ever wondered how Jesus responded to people? What was He thinking as He scanned the sea of faces around Him? Verses 35–38 give us an enlightening look through His eyes—a look we can use to guide our own approach to evangelizing the people around us.

The Scene through Jesus' Eyes

For the moment, Jesus sidesteps a fight with the Pharisees to get on with the more important work of ministering to the people.

> And Jesus was going about all the cities and the villages, teaching in their synagogues, and proclaiming the gospel of the kingdom, and healing every kind of disease and every kind of sickness. (v. 35)

From morning to night, in city after city, Jesus bandages the wounds of a despairing nation. He cleanses lepers, lifts fevers, feeds stomachs, and nourishes souls. And still they keep coming—a mother, weeping over her sick baby; a father, carrying his lame son. Bearing burdens on their backs and fears in their hearts, they come to Jesus as refugees of a fallen world.

At some point, Jesus steps back and surveys the crowd of lost, broken lives. Just then, Matthew snaps a picture of Him and later records it for us in verse 36. Here we see not the face of a man overwhelmed by the task ahead but the face of God moved to tears by the depth of human suffering.

The Nature of Jesus' Compassion

> And seeing the multitudes, He felt compassion for them, because they were distressed and downcast like sheep without a shepherd. (v. 36)

The compassion of Jesus is the undergirding to any evangelistic bridge we might hope to build. Without it, our efforts to reach the lost crumble. So let's take a moment to understand the concept of "compassion" in this verse.

The Greek word is a tongue twister: *splagchnizomai*. This verb's original root meant "the inward parts," which the ancients regarded as the site of human feelings. The word later took on a figurative meaning, defining the powerful natural passions that churn within us—anger, love, desire. Jewish and Christian writers choose it as the perfect word to mean not passion but *compassion*.

The verb form plays a special role in the New Testament. It appears nowhere but in the gospels and is used only of Jesus or by Jesus in His parables—the good Samaritan feels compassion for the victim (Luke 10:33); the father, for his prodigal son (15:20).[1] Compassion combines the Christian ideals of love and mercy.

So, in saying that Jesus felt compassion for the people, Matthew meant more than He felt sorry for them. He meant that Jesus' heart ached for them, as a father's heart might ache for his suffering children and compel him to sacrifice everything to save them. Compassion is an action, full of purpose and energy. It's the fuel that burned within Jesus, driving His entire life and mission.

The Reason for Jesus' Compassion

What moved Jesus so deeply? Matthew 9:36 gives the reason: "because they were distressed and downcast like sheep without a shepherd." Like a scattered flock, the people were wandering into all sorts of dangers—a deep pit, a treacherous canyon, the jaws of vicious wolves.

The Greek word for *distressed* is vivid, as commentator Alfred Plummer tells us:

> Originally it meant "flayed" or "mangled," but became equivalent to "harassed" or "vexed" with weariness or worry.[2]

Tormented and bewildered, they were victims of a world system (and a religious system) that was tearing their souls apart, and they had no one to lead them to safety.

They were *downcast* as well. Plummer pictures them as "exhausted in the vain search for pasture."[3] Does that describe some of the people you know? They've searched everywhere for the green pastures of happiness—in education, career, pleasure, and possessions. They may even have looked for it in a bottle of alcohol or

---

1. See "splanchna," in *The New International Dictionary of New Testament Theology*, Colin Brown, gen. ed. (Grand Rapids, Mich.: Zondervan Publishing House, Regency Reference Library, 1976), vol. 2, p. 599.

2. Alfred Plummer, *An Exegetical Commentary on the Gospel according to St. Matthew* (London, England: Robert Scott Roxburghe House, Paternoster Row, 1909), p. 145, n. 1.

3. Plummer, *Matthew*, p. 145.

a syringeful of drugs. For all their searching, though, they found no cool springs or soft meadows, only brambles and dust. And now there's a weariness in their eyes that reaches down to the soul. That's what Jesus saw in the people around Him. And it broke His heart.

The Action Jesus Took

Jesus cannot stand by and do nothing. But what He does may surprise you.

> Then He said to His disciples, "The harvest is plentiful, but the workers are few. Therefore beseech the Lord of the harvest to send out workers into His harvest." (vv. 37–38)

The spiritual fruit is falling off the vine. People are ripe for the gospel. "So," Jesus says, "pray."

Pray? We'd expect Him to say, "Get busy!" But He doesn't. He knows the size of the task and the strength of the enemy. To get the job done, God must send out His people filled with His power and bearing His authority. And that's just what Jesus does.

> And having summoned His twelve disciples, He gave them authority over unclean spirits, to cast them out, and to heal every kind of disease and every kind of sickness. . . .
> These twelve Jesus sent out after instructing them, saying, "Do not go in the way of the Gentiles, and do not enter any city of the Samaritans; but rather go to the lost sheep of the house of Israel." (10:1, 5–6)

Matthew also lists the names of the disciples (vv. 2–4), perhaps to remind us that God uses ordinary people. None of the Twelve had seminary degrees or ministry experience. They were garden-variety folks who were willing to become instruments in the Master's hand.

Putting Ourselves into the Scene

Sometimes we make evangelism more complicated than necessary. We can worry so much about getting the technique right that we lose the heart of Christ. Thinking through His example, let's cull four essentials that will make our efforts to evangelize more natural.

First, *we must see clearly.* Though needs pressed in all around

Him, Jesus took the time to really see the people He ministered to. They weren't numbers or duties to accomplish. They were individuals with hearts and souls—eternal souls. We, too, must see as Jesus saw if we're to be effective for Him. We must break out of our preoccupied mind-sets and look beyond our daily concerns. Then we will discover the people around us and notice their gifts and needs, maybe for the first time.

Second, *we must feel deeply.* Before He said anything to His disciples, Jesus first felt the depth of the people's pain. We also must be willing to stand with others in their hurt and confusion. Try putting yourself in other people's shoes. What would it be like to think you couldn't make it through the day without a drink? What would it feel like for your spouse to leave you after fifteen years of marriage? Try to empathize and connect, to care about what others are going through.

Third, *we must pray specifically.* Jesus wanted His disciples to pray for sensitive, capable workers for the harvest. And part of being that kind of worker means taking care of others through prayer. Prayer is the most important aspect of evangelism—yet it's the easiest to overlook. Do you know just three people you could uphold in prayer? Start kneeling today, and watch God's grace go to work.

Fourth, *we must go willingly.* Matthew doesn't record a single sign of reluctance among the disciples when Jesus sent them out. This is where we put our faith to work. Where we move from feeling sorry for people to feeling Christ's compassion for them. God may send us as His workers, but He won't go for us. He may open the door, but only we can walk through it. The decision is ours. Are we willing to go?

 Living Insights

Seeing people clearly, without the blur of preconceived notions, can dramatically change how we relate to them. Stephen Covey, author of *The Seven Habits of Highly Effective People,* experienced the power of "corrected vision" on a New York subway.

> People were sitting quietly—some reading newspapers, some lost in thought, some resting with their eyes closed. It was a calm, peaceful scene.
> Then suddenly, a man and his children entered

the subway car. The children were so loud and rambunctious that instantly the whole climate changed.

The man sat down next to me and closed his eyes, apparently oblivious to the situation. The children were yelling back and forth, throwing things, even grabbing people's papers. It was very disturbing. And yet, the man sitting next to me did nothing.

It was difficult not to feel irritated. I could not believe that he could be so insensitive as to let his children run wild like that and do nothing about it, taking no responsibility at all. It was easy to see that everyone else on the subway felt irritated, too. So finally, with what I felt was unusual patience and restraint, I turned to him and said, "Sir, your children are really disturbing a lot of people. I wonder if you couldn't control them a little more?"

The man lifted his gaze as if to come to a consciousness of the situation for the first time and said softly, "Oh, you're right. I guess I should do something about it. We just came from the hospital where their mother died about an hour ago. I don't know what to think, and I guess they don't know how to handle it either."

Can you imagine what I felt at that moment?
. . . Suddenly I *saw* things differently, and because I *saw* differently, I *thought* differently, I *felt* differently, I *behaved* differently. My irritation vanished. I didn't have to worry about controlling my attitude or my behavior; my heart was filled with the man's pain.[4]

So often, we rush to make judgments about people—particularly the unsaved. We look at them, but we don't really see them. We don't see their hearts . . . or their hurts.

Think of an unsaved person you know. Do you understand what's going on beneath the surface of his or her life?

Are you willing to find out?

---

4. Stephen R. Covey, *The Seven Habits of Highly Effective People* (New York, N.Y.: Simon and Schuster, A Fireside Book, 1989), pp. 30–31.

Chapter 9

No Sowing—No Reaping
Galatians 6:7–10

A man from the city decided he'd had enough of the honking traffic, sooty skies, and gray concrete. So he packed his things and moved into a little red farmhouse on a few acres in the country.

Each morning, he'd fill his lungs with the clean country air, pull on a pair of comfy overalls, and listen to the sweet chirping of birds. "This is living!" he'd say to himself as he sipped his coffee.

One day he heard a knock on the door. It was his nearest neighbor from ten miles away.

"Howdy," drawled the neighbor.

"Hello," said the man cheerily. He was glad to have company.

"Brought you a housewarmin' present," said the neighbor, who plopped down a dusty burlap sack filled with what looked like sand.

"Th-thank you," said the man, somewhat taken aback.

"Well, can't stand around gabbin' all day," said the neighbor. And he tipped his straw hat and walked away.

The city dweller scratched his head and looked at the sack. "A gift is a gift," he said to himself, "no matter how odd." He figured he'd better find some use for it, so he dragged it over to the back door. "A genuine country doorstop," he said, admiring the new addition to his home.

Months passed, and the man decided to visit his farmer friend. Ascending the hill that separated the properties, he stopped at the crest. Before him was the most beautiful sight he'd ever seen. His neighbor's farmhouse sat like a jewel in the center of a golden carpet of wheat fields spreading out in all directions. The man hurried down the hill to speak to the farmer.

"I wish I had a farm like yours," said the man in awe. "My property grows nothing but weeds."

The farmer eyed him carefully. "Whadya do with the seed I brought you?"

"Was that seed?" asked the man sheepishly. "I . . . I used it for a doorstop."

The farmer's mouth drew up in a grin, and he laughed until his sides hurt. "Son, seed ain't no good unless you spread it around!

The first thing you need to learn about being a farmer is this: If you wanna reap, you gotta sow."

The Laws of the Harvest

That's a good lesson for all of us to remember, whether we're city slickers or country folks. We can apply it to every area of life. Take finances, for example. If we don't invest when we're young, we won't reap when we're old. Or education. If we don't study hard in school, we won't have the edge in our career. And in the area of evangelism, if we don't sow the gospel in people's lives, we won't reap a spiritual harvest.

We can learn a lot about sowing and reaping from Paul's words in Galatians 6:7–10. From his counsel, we can glean a few principles to guide us as we spread the good news of Christ. Let's call them "laws of the harvest."[1]

Law 1: We Reap Only What Has Been Sown

> Do not be deceived, God is not mocked; for what-
> ever a man sows, this he will also reap. (Gal. 6:7)

Every harvest has to begin as seed. There's no such thing as spontaneous generation—something coming from nothing. Have you ever had a vegetable garden suddenly sprout on your front lawn? Not unless, for some strange reason, you threw some seeds out there!

The same principle operates in the spiritual realm too. Whatever we reap was planted by either God or people, as Paul reminded the Corinthian believers: "I planted, Apollos watered, but God was causing the growth" (1 Cor. 3:6). The Corinthians' faith didn't grow from nothing. Paul and Apollos sowed and nourished the seed of God's Word, and God made it blossom in their lives.

When it comes to our salvation, we find that God has done all the sowing for us. Out of His love, He sent His Son to die on the cross; and by simply believing in Christ's finished work, we reap the bountiful harvest of eternal life (see John 3:16). We don't have to work for it. We don't have to earn it. We just need to receive it. That's the essence of the news we share with the world.

---

1. This chapter is based on John W. Lawrence's book *Life's Choices: Discovering the Consequences of Sowing and Reaping* (Portland, Oreg.: Multnomah Press, 1975), in which he presents seven laws of the harvest.

Law 2: We Reap the Same in Kind as We Sow

This second law is a corollary to the first—if we plant, we'll reap; and what we plant, we'll reap. If we plant radish seeds, for example, we'll reap radishes. Spiritually speaking, if we plant seeds of integrity, we'll reap good character.

Some people, however, think it doesn't matter what kind of seeds they sow. For years they freely scatter seeds of pride, dishonesty, and anger. Then they're shocked when they begin to reap the bitter consequences—a longtime business partnership crumbles, a legal suit is filed, a marriage ends in divorce. Truly, as one of Job's counselors observed,

> "According to what I have seen, those who plow
> iniquity
> And those who sow trouble harvest it." (Job 4:8)

Paul put it this way: "The one who sows to his own flesh shall from the flesh reap corruption" (Gal. 6:8a). Thankfully, however, there's a positive side as well: "The one who sows to the Spirit shall from the Spirit reap eternal life" (v. 8b).

Many parents have witnessed this in their homes. Here and there, they drop little seeds of faith in the lives of their children. After a while, a fragile shoot breaks the surface. Then buds of godliness emerge and blossom. In time, the children start to bear fruit on their branches and reproduce their faith in the lives of others. It's a thrilling sight for any parent to see.

Law 3: We Reap More and in a Different Season Than We Sow

We glean the third law from verses 9–10:

> And let us not lose heart in doing good, for in due
> time we shall reap if we do not grow weary. So then,
> while we have opportunity, let us do good to all men,
> and especially to those who are of the household of
> the faith.

This law has two components. First, *we reap more than we sow*. Each tiny seed is a storehouse of enormous potential, for either good or evil. For a small investment of a few sacks of seed, a farmer can reap a silo of grain—a return of a hundredfold. If only our financial investments paid off as well! On the other hand, we wouldn't really want our harmful habits to produce an even greater yield of destruction. As Solomon wrote,

> He who sows iniquity will reap vanity [trouble, sorrow]. (Prov. 22:8)

David discovered the destructive power of one seed of sin sown in secret. A lingering look at Bathsheba sprouted into a lustful thought, which grew into a thorny bramble of adultery, an unexpected pregnancy, and murder. Tragically, the tendrils from that thorn bush kept growing, entangling his entire family. In uncontrolled lust, David's son Amnon raped his half sister, Tamar. Another son, Absalom, killed Amnon in revenge, then tried to take over his father's kingdom. David spent the rest of his days reaping the bitter harvest from that one seed of sin. To borrow Hosea's words, he sowed the wind and reaped the whirlwind (see Hos. 8:7).

Just as a little sin can produce great evil, so can a little bit of God's kingdom planted in our lives produce enormous good. Jesus told us,

> "The kingdom of heaven is like a mustard seed, which a man took and sowed in his field; and this is smaller than all other seeds; but when it is full grown, it is larger than the garden plants, and becomes a tree, so that the birds of the air come and nest in its branches." (Matt. 13:31–32)

We benefit many times over what we've sown, and so do others as they find safety and shelter in our godly character.

The second component to this law is, *we reap in a different season than we sow*. We think good deeds should be rewarded right away. Like children, we impatiently dig up a seed we just planted to see if it's doing anything. However, magic beans excluded, seeds don't grow overnight. Paul says to us, "*in due time* we shall reap" (Gal. 6:9, emphasis added).

Farmers run their lives by that principle. They sow in one season with a view toward a future season. They see today as an opportunity to invest for tomorrow. They patiently live for the long-term reward. Do you live that way? Are you content to wait for Christ's rewards? Are you willing to sow seeds of righteousness now in order to yield a bountiful harvest later?

Law 4: We Reap the Full Harvest of Good Only If We Persevere

Because the harvest is future, as wise spiritual farmers we must stick to the hard work of tilling and sowing today. Even when we don't see the results of our labors, Paul encourages us, "Let us not lose heart in doing good, for in due time we shall reap if we do not grow weary" (v. 9).

The devil will come alongside us and use discouragement to pull our hands from the plow. He'll say, "Look how hard you're working, and for what? You've got dirt on your face. Calluses on your hands. And a field full of nothing. You couldn't grow a bean sprout! So why try? Don't waste your life. Take it easy. Live a little. You deserve better than this!"

But the Lord holds a vision of the harvest before us and urges us to persevere. "You *shall* reap," He promises, "if you do not grow weary." We will enter heaven with our arms laden with the rich rewards of our faith. But it means that we must do three things during this season of earthly life:

1. Keep making the right decisions, no matter the opposition we may run into.

2. Keep taking the right actions, no matter how difficult or unpopular that may be.

3. Keep modeling Christ to others, no matter how tempted we may be to do otherwise.

Conclusion

Never underestimate the power of sowing the right seeds. Sometimes we think that a small act of love or a brief word of hope won't make much difference. But God can take that tiny seed of truth in a person's heart and grow a fruitful vine of faith.

> "For as the rain and the snow come down from
>   heaven,
> And do not return there without watering the earth,
> And making it bear and sprout,
> And furnishing seed to the sower and bread to
>   the eater;
> So shall My word be which goes forth from My mouth;
> It shall not return to Me empty,
> Without accomplishing what I desire,
> And without succeeding in the matter for which I
>   sent it." (Isa. 55:10–11)

Living Insights

Farmers don't make the seed grow. They simply create the right conditions for growth. They cultivate the soil, irrigate it, and sow the seed. The sun, the rain, and God do the rest.

Similarly, we don't make the gospel take root in people's hearts. We just cultivate the relationship and plant the seeds of truth; God causes the growth.

Perhaps you've been cultivating a relationship with an unbeliever, and now you're ready to sow some seeds. But you worry that you might turn the person off or say the wrong thing, and he or she will be lost forever. That God causes the seed to grow is one of the most freeing facts to remember. Certainly, we must strive to be considerate and clear in our witnessing. But we mustn't think that a person's salvation depends on our technique.

From the following verses, what role do the members of the Trinity have in bringing a person to salvation?

The Father—John 6:44; 2 Thessalonians 2:13: _____

_____

The Son—John 12:32: _____

_____

The Holy Spirit—John 16:7–14: _____

_____

Are you able to release your unsaved friend into God's hands?

_____

_____

Maybe you've tried sowing seeds in an unsaved person's life and nothing has happened. It's hard to be patient, isn't it? But you can't rush the harvest. Take a moment to reread Isaiah 55:10–11. What thoughts can you glean from these verses to help you not give up on this person?

_____

Waiting on God doesn't mean we have to stop sowing seeds. Who knows when one of them will take root, maybe not now but in the future in a different situation? So be encouraged in your evangelism efforts. And remember that Christ is the Lord of the harvest.

Chapter 10

NO FOLLOW-UP—
NO FOLLOW-THROUGH
Luke 24:13–35

Babies are big business.

Parents in America alone collectively spend millions of dollars each year to keep their little ones cooing with contentment. There are bottles to buy, as well as bibs, bouncers, and baby toys. A rocker is nice, and a crib is a must. So is a changing table, fully stocked with everything you need to keep your baby's bottom in the pink. You should see all the gels, powders, and ointments available on the baby aisle in the market . . . as well as the smorgasbord of diapers. There are diapers for girls and diapers for boys. Trim-fitting and heavy-duty. Tape and Velcro. Did you know that the average baby from birth to age two goes through about three thousand disposable diapers? At half an inch thick, the diapers would make a stack twelve stories high!

Despite the high cost of babies, parents keep having them. What makes moms and dads willing to pay the price? A touch of insanity, perhaps? No, mostly a lot of love and a large measure of hope for the future.

Caring for newborn Christians requires a similar level of commitment and vision. It's one thing to take part in the labor and delivery of a baby believer, but it's quite another thing to nurture that new life into maturity.

Evangelism: What It Is . . . and Isn't

Evangelism is like obstetrics. It emphasizes birth, not growth. Its goal is to deliver healthy baby Christians, not take care of newborns. That's the job of the church. Consequently, the scope of an evangelistic message is limited. It focuses on the gospel, not on detailed theology.

Sometimes evangelists are criticized because they stay in the shallows of theology and rarely plunge into the depths. But we have to consider their audience—unsaved people who are just testing the spiritual waters.

Some churches make the mistake of pushing non-Christians into the theological deep end before they're ready. Perhaps you've heard the story of the visitor who said to his Sunday school teacher, "I'm struggling a bit with Genesis." Immediately, the teacher launched into a discussion of the latest theories on authorship and textual sources. When he was through, the visitor replied, "That's nice, but I'm having trouble finding Genesis."

At the other extreme, some churches preach only the basic salvation message, even to Christians. Every Sunday service is an evangelistic crusade. Occasionally people get saved, but how can they grow on a constant diet of the milk of the gospel?

It's best to view the church not primarily as an arena for evangelism but as a center for worship, teaching, and fellowship, where Christians can refuel for the task of evangelizing during the week. Christ designed His church to be a warm, learning environment—the perfect place for rearing healthy spiritual babies.

Follow-up: What It Does Include . . . and Doesn't

A baby's first year after birth is just as critical as the nine months before birth. Will her immune system function properly? Will his heart beat with a healthy rhythm? A baby believer's first year is also as critical. Will his faith resist temptation? Will her love for Christ keep growing?

Like pediatricians, who follow up newborns to give them a healthy start in life, we need to follow up new believers to help them follow through with their commitment to Christ. This requires a special touch—the kind of touch Jesus displayed as He conversed with two travelers on the road to Emmaus.

The story takes place on the heels of the Passion Week. Shaken to the core by the sight of their Savior on the cross, Jesus' followers have just received a second blow with the news that His tomb is empty. With their faith in turmoil, two of His followers set out from Jerusalem to their home in Emmaus to sort it all out.

> And they were conversing with each other about all these things which had taken place. And it came about that while they were conversing and discussing, Jesus Himself approached, and began traveling with them. But their eyes were prevented from recognizing Him. (Luke 24:14–16)

Don't you love the intrigue of this moment? They think He's dead, but He's walking right beside them!

> And He said to them, "What are these words that you are exchanging with one another as you are walking?" And they stood still, looking sad. And one of them, named Cleopas, answered and said to Him, "Are You the only one visiting Jerusalem and unaware of the things which have happened here in these days?" And He said to them, "What things?" (vv. 17–19a)

Jesus could clear up their confusion by revealing Himself, but He doesn't. Why? Because He knows that their faith won't develop any muscle if He spoon-feeds them all the answers. They need to unload the burden on their hearts and grapple with the issues themselves. So, to help them grow, He holds back His identity and asks a few questions.

There's a great temptation to do all the talking when we're following up with a new believer. The itch to pull out the charts and spout all the truth we've learned over the past thirty years is almost unbearable. Our knowledge may impress young believers, but it doesn't teach them anything except to depend on us rather than dig for their own answers. From Jesus' example, we learn the first principle of follow-up:

> *Graciously ask a few questions*
> *rather than dogmatically giving all the answers.*

Jesus' questions provide a window into the men's thinking.

> And they said to Him, "The things about Jesus the Nazarene, who was a prophet mighty in deed and word in the sight of God and all the people, and how the chief priests and our rulers delivered Him up to the sentence of death, and crucified Him. But we were hoping that it was He who was going to redeem Israel. Indeed, besides all this, it is the third day since these things happened. But also some women among us amazed us. When they were at the tomb early in the morning, and did not find His body, they came, saying that they had also seen a vision of angels, who said that He was alive. And

73

some of those who were with us went to the tomb
and found it just exactly as the women also had said;
but Him they did not see." (vv. 19b–24)

During this lengthy account, Jesus is doing something extremely important—He's listening. He's sensing their tone of voice. He's reading hand gestures and facial expressions. He's letting the two have full control of the conversation, without interrupting. Even when they say, "We were hoping that it was He who was going to redeem Israel," Jesus doesn't jump in to correct them.

What emotion does Jesus hear? One clue is in verse 11. Mary Magdalene and the other women had just rushed back from the empty tomb, out of breath and bursting with the news that Jesus was alive.

And these words appeared to them as nonsense, and
they would not believe them.

Dead people don't get up and walk away from their own tombs. *That's nonsense!* Jesus couldn't be alive . . . could He?

Jesus must have felt the tremors of doubt quaking their faith. We, too, need to be sensitive to the doubts that invariably shake new believers. Having just emerged from years of unbelief, their perspectives and habits may shock us. However, we need to allow them space to test their new faith. Remember, it's God's job to firm their footing and clean up their lives; it's our job to love them through the process. The principle we glean is this:

Patiently listen for hints of doubt
rather than controlling the conversation.

What anchor does God use to strengthen a new believer's faith? Jesus shows us in verses 25–27:

And He said to them, "O foolish men and slow of heart to believe in all that the prophets have spoken! Was it not necessary for the Christ to suffer these things and to enter into His glory?" And beginning with Moses and with all the prophets, He explained to them the things concerning Himself in all the Scriptures.

Seeing the men awash in a whirlpool of questions and fears, Jesus firmly sets them on the rock of Scripture, as He reveals God's plan of redemption from the beginning.

New Christians often wrestle with their emotions: "I don't feel like a different person. Is this real or just wishful thinking? Does God still love me?" An open Bible can work wonders in calming their fears. Bedrock verses about Christ and the unchanging character of God, His mercy, His love, His forgiveness give new believers a firm foundation. They're used to living by their experiences—"If it feels good, do it." We must encourage them to live by God's Word—"If it says so, believe it." So, when following up a new Christian,

Confidently and thoroughly instruct in the Scripture rather than focusing on feelings and experience.

On the road to Emmaus, the miles fly by as Christ unveils the mysteries of the Scriptures. Soon the travelers arrive at their destination.

> And they approached the village where they were going, and He acted as though He would go farther. And they urged Him, saying, "Stay with us, for it is getting toward evening, and the day is now nearly over." And He went in to stay with them. (vv. 28–29)

Exhibiting the gracious style that characterized His earthly ministry, Jesus enters their homes and their lives by their invitation. We can show that same personal touch to new Christians by not being pushy, by waiting to be invited to spend time with them over a cup of coffee. By entering their homes and sharing a meal. By being available to talk. In all these ways, we model Christ's love and put flesh on what it means to be a Christian. This is the other side of evangelism. This is discipleship—people inspiring others by their example to live for Christ. We can state the principle like this:

Faithfully stay available instead of remaining aloof.

At the dinner table, Jesus unveils His true identity:

> And it came about that when He had reclined at the table with them, He took the bread and blessed it, and breaking it, He began giving it to them. And their eyes were opened and they recognized Him; and He vanished from their sight. (vv. 30–31)

Perhaps the way He distributed the bread tipped them off that He was Jesus, or maybe the men noticed the nail scars on His hands. Either way, they finally *recognized* Him. The Greek word is *epiginōskō*, which means to "fully perceive"; it is "a knowledge 'which perfectly unites the subject with the object.'"[1]

The men "connected" with Jesus. This is the goal of follow-up, to display Christ to people so that they fall deeper in love with Him. He is the focus of attention, not us. And the more they grow dependent on Him, the less they need us. Discipleship, like parenting, is a letting-go process. This brings us to our final principle on follow-up:

Consistently model Christ rather than promoting yourself.

For these men, the road to Emmaus was a thrilling journey of faith that started in doubt and fear and ended in an encounter with Jesus. The story concludes with the two men running back to Jerusalem that same night, full of faith and proclaiming, "The Lord has really risen, and has appeared to Simon" (v. 34).

Involvement: What to Remember . . . and Forget

Let's pull together these thoughts about nurturing newborn believers with three things to remember and three things to forget.

First, *remember that new Christians are newborns, so forget frequent acts of immaturity.* They may desire to walk tall, but their wobbly legs won't let them. They'll make grand promises and break them. They'll agree to meet with you, then forget the appointment. They'll make a commitment, then lapse into their old lifestyle. When they do, forgive them, and don't try to manipulate them into good behavior. Accountability is OK; oppression is not.

Second, *remember that they can be demanding, so forget about being rewarded.* New believers are sometimes so focused on getting their lives together that they neglect to say, "Thank you." We have to keep in mind that we are the servants. Our job is to wash their feet with acts of grace and acceptance, and let God give the rewards.

Third, *remember that they are easily persuaded, so forget about impressing them with your own importance.* At the other extreme, some new Christians will give too much praise. They'll try to put you on a pedestal and think that your words fall directly from God's lips. Give them a regular diet of humanity. Let them know about your struggles. Remind them that you're on the same journey they are and you're learning too.

---

1. W. E. Vine, *Vine's Expository Dictionary of Old and New Testament Words,* Old Testament edited by F. F. Bruce (Old Tappan, N.J.: Fleming H. Revell Co., 1981), p. 299.

A Final Word

We know how to find the babies at church; we just listen for the crying and head toward the nursery. However, it's not that easy to spot the spiritual babies. They're crying too, but not audibly. They're crying for spiritual support and guidance, for someone to show them that Christ's love is real. Won't you consider adopting a spiritual baby? It's true, the price is high. But, as any parent will tell you, it's worth it.

 Living Insights STUDY ONE

Are you prepared to be a spiritual parent? Caring for babies is a time-consuming and sometimes messy job. Should you decide to adopt, the principles from our study can help you evaluate the areas that might need attention. As you reflect on them, place an X on the scale to indicate whether you tend toward the positive or the negative side.

Principle 1: Graciously ask a few questions rather than dogmatically giving all the answers.

1 2 3 4 5 6 7 8 9 10

I tend to graciously ask a few questions.   *I tend to give all the answers.*

Principle 2: Patiently listen for hints of doubt rather than controlling the conversation.

1 2 3 4 5 6 7 8 9 10

I tend to patiently listen.   *I tend to control the conversation.*

Principle 3: Confidently and thoroughly instruct in the Scripture rather than focusing on feelings and experience.

1 2 3 4 5 6 7 8 9 10

I tend to confidently and thoroughly   *I tend to focus on feelings and experience.*
instruct in the Scripture.

Principle 4: Faithfully stay available instead of remaining aloof.

1 2 3 4 5 6 7 8 9 10

I tend to faithfully stay available.   *I tend to remain aloof.*

Principle 5: Consistently model Christ rather than promoting yourself.

1 2 3 4 5 6 7 8 9 10

I tend to consistently model Christ.   *I tend to promote myself.*

What is one area about yourself that you need to improve to become a spiritual parent?

_____

_____

_____

Just as no one can be totally prepared for parenthood, no one can be completely ready to disciple a new Christian. But then, we don't need to be perfect, just growing. Do you know a young believer you could take under your wing? Who is this person?

_____

Making the first contact is often the hardest. When you're ready, give this person a call. Set up your first appointment. It could be that you're the one he or she has been longing to meet.

Living Insights   STUDY TWO

In this study, we've looked at evangelism from many angles. Like a marble sculpture in a garden, the subject takes on different shapes as we circle around it. As you think back on the various chapters, which perspective meant the most to you?

_____

_____

_____

How has this new perspective helped you relate better to non-Christians?

_____

_____

_____

In what ways have you seen your compassion for the lost grow deeper?

_____

_____

_____

What is the one thing you can do as a result of this study that will keep your mind-set focused on evangelism?

_____

_____

_____

What other ways can we look at evangelism? The resources listed in the Books for Probing Further section will show you many more facets. Each perspective offers new and fascinating insights. Evangelism, according to God's design, is truly a work of art.

BOOKS FOR PROBING FURTHER

I f this study has gotten your evangelistic juices flowing, the following resources for both you and your church should help satisfy your appetite. Dig into one that looks good to you, and enjoy.

Evangelism Foundations

Aldrich, Joseph C. *Life-Style Evangelism.* Portland, Oreg.: Multnomah Press, 1981.

Coleman, Robert E. *The Master Plan of Evangelism.* Grand Rapids, Mich.: Baker Book House, Fleming H. Revell Co., 1993.

Pippert, Rebecca Manley. *Out of the Saltshaker and into the World.* Downers Grove, Ill.: InterVarsity Press, 1979.

Evangelism How-Tos

Aldrich, Joseph C. *Gentle Persuasion: Creative Ways to Introduce Your Friends to Christ.* Portland, Oreg.: Multnomah Press, 1988.

Eims, LeRoy. *One-to-One Evangelism.* Wheaton, Ill.: Scripture Press Publications, Victor Books, 1990. This is an enlarged and updated version of the original book *Winning Ways.*

Jacks, Bob and Betty, with Ron Wormser, Sr. *Your Home a Lighthouse.* Rev. ed. Colorado Springs, Colo.: NavPress, 1987.

Kramp, John. *Out of Their Faces and into Their Shoes.* Nashville, Tenn.: Broadman and Holman Publishers, 1995.

Little, Paul E. *How to Give Away Your Faith.* Downers Grove, Ill.: InterVarsity Press, 1966.

Petersen, Jim. *Living Proof.* Colorado Springs, Colo.: NavPress, 1989. Originally published in two books: *Evangelism as a Lifestyle* (1980) and *Evangelism for Our Generation* (1985). Video curriculum available.

Sweeting, George. *The No-Guilt Guide to Witnessing.* Wheaton, Ill.: Scripture Press Publications, Victor Books, 1991.

Evangelism Ideas

Campolo, Tony, and Gordon Aeschliman. *50 Ways You Can Share Your Faith*. Downers Grove, Ill.: InterVarsity Press, 1992.

Moyer, Larry, and Cameron D. Abell, eds. *142 Evangelism Ideas for Your Church*. Grand Rapids, Mich.: Baker Book House, 1990.

Evangelism Resources for Your Pastor

Barna, George. *Evangelism That Works*. Ventura, Calif.: Gospel Light, Regal Books, 1995.

Loscalzo, Craig A. *Evangelistic Preaching That Connects*. Downers Grove, Ill.: InterVarsity Press, 1995.

Search Ministries. 5038 Dorsey Hall Drive, Ellicott City, MD 21042. (410) 740-5300. This ministry provides evangelism training and consulting as well as the excellent publication *Common Ground*.

Evangelism Tracts and Publications

"How to Have a Happy and Meaningful Life." Dallas Theological Seminary, 3909 Swiss Avenue, Dallas, TX 75204. (214) 824-3094.

Pursuit. Evangelical Free Church of America. 901 East 78th Street, Minneapolis, MN 55420. (800) 995-5360. Designed for the non-Christian who is interested in spiritual matters, this magazine provides a bridge to a discussion about Christ.

"Your Most Important Relationship." Campus Crusade for Christ International, San Bernardino, CA 92414.

Some of these books may be out of print and available only through a library. For those currently available, please contact your local Christian bookstore. Books by Charles R. Swindoll may be obtained through Insight for Living. IFL also offers some books by other authors—please note the ordering information that follows and contact the office that serves you.

ORDERING INFORMATION

GOD'S WORD, GOD'S WORLD . . . AND YOU
Cassette Tapes and Study Guide

This Bible study guide was designed to be used independently or in conjunction with the broadcast of Chuck Swindoll's taped messages which are listed below. If you would like to order cassette tapes or further copies of this study guide, please see the information given below and the order form provided at the end of this guide.

		U.S.	Canada
GWY	Study guide	$ 4.95	$ 6.50
GWYCS	Cassette series, includes all individual tapes, album cover, and one complimentary study guide	25.95	37.25
GWY 1–5	Individual cassettes, includes messages A and B	6.00	7.48

Prices are subject to change without notice.

GWY 1-A: *God's Strange Change Plan*—Selected Scriptures
     B: *Sharing the Good News as a Church*—Survey of Acts

GWY 2-A: *Taking Advantage of Today's Advantages*—Luke 10:25–37
     B: *A Nonexclusive Covenant*—Selected Scriptures

GWY 3-A: *Strengthening Your Grip on Evangelism*—Acts 8:26–39
     B: *"Mr Smith, Meet Your Substitute"*—Selected Scriptures

GWY 4-A: *No Repentance—No Revival*—Selected Scriptures
     B: *No Compassion—No Harvest*—Matthew 9:27–10:5

GWY 5-A: *No Sowing—No Reaping*—Galatians 6:7–10
     B: *No Follow-Up—No Follow-Through*—Luke 24:13–35

HOW TO ORDER BY PHONE OR FAX
(Credit card orders only)

Web site: http://www.insight.org

United States: 1-800-772-8888 or FAX (714) 575-5684, 24 hours a day, 7 days a week

Canada: 1-800-663-7639 or FAX (604) 532-7173, 24 hours a day, 7 days a week

Australia and the South Pacific: (03) 9877-4277 from 8:00 A.M. to 5:00 P.M., Monday through Friday.
FAX (03) 9877-4077 anytime, day or night

Other International Locations: call the International Ordering Services Department in the United States at (714) 575-5000 from 8:00 A.M. to 4:30 P.M., Pacific time, Monday through Friday
FAX (714) 575-5683 anytime, day or night

HOW TO ORDER BY MAIL

United States
• Mail to: Mail Center
           Insight for Living
           Post Office Box 69000
           Anaheim, CA 92817-0900
• Sales tax: California residents add 7.75%. Texas residents add 8.25%.
• Shipping and handling charges must be added to each order. See chart on order form for amount.
• Payment: personal checks, money orders, credit cards (Visa, MasterCard, Discover Card, and American Express). No invoices or COD orders available.
• $10 fee for *any* returned check.

Canada
• Mail to: Insight for Living Ministries
           Post Office Box 2510
           Vancouver, BC V6B 3W7
• Sales tax: please add 7% GST. British Columbia residents also add 7% sales tax (on tapes or cassette series).
• Shipping and handling charges must be added to each order. See chart on order form for amount.
• Payment: personal cheques, money orders, credit cards (Visa, Master-Card). No invoices or COD orders available.
• Delivery: approximately four weeks.

Australia and the South Pacific
• Mail to: Insight for Living, Inc.
           GPO Box 2823 EE
           Melbourne, Victoria 3001, Australia

- Shipping: add 25% to the total order.
- Delivery: approximately four to six weeks.
- Payment: personal checks payable in Australian funds, international money orders, or credit cards (Visa, MasterCard, and Bankcard).

United Kingdom and Europe
- Mail to: Insight for Living
            c/o Trans World Radio
            Post Office Box 1020
            Bristol BS99 1XS
            England, United Kingdom
- Shipping: add 25% to the total order.
- Delivery: approximately four to six weeks.
- Payment: cheques payable in sterling pounds or credit cards (Visa, MasterCard, and American Express).

Other International Locations
- Mail to: International Processing Services Department
            Insight for Living
            Post Office Box 69000
            Anaheim, CA 92817-0900
- Shipping and delivery time: please see chart that follows.
- Payment: personal checks payable in U.S. funds, international money orders, or credit cards (Visa, MasterCard, and American Express).

Type of Shipping	Postage Cost	Delivery
Surface	10% of total order*	6 to 10 weeks
Airmail	25% of total order*	under 6 weeks

*Use U.S. price as a base.

Our Guarantee: Your complete satisfaction is our top priority here at Insight for Living. If you're not completely satisfied with anything you order, please return it for full credit, a refund, or a replacement, as you prefer.

Insight for Living Catalog: The Insight for Living catalog features study guides, tapes, and books by a variety of Christian authors. To obtain a free copy, call us at the numbers listed above.

Order Form
United States, Australia, and Other International Locations
(Canadian residents please use order form on reverse side.)

GWYCS represents the entire *God's Word, God's World . . . and You* series in a special album cover, while GWY 1–5 are the individual tapes included in the series. GWY represents this study guide, should you desire to order additional copies.

Product Code	Product Description	Qty.	Price	Total
GWY	Study Guide		$ 4.95	$
GWYCS	Casette Series with study guide		25.95	
GWY-	Individual cassette		6.00	
GWY-	Individual cassette		6.00	
GWY-	Individual cassette		6.00	

Order Total

UPS ❑   First Class ❑
Shipping and handling must be added. See chart for charges.

Amount of Order	First Class	UPS
$ 7.50 and under	1.00	4.00
$ 7.51 to 12.50	1.50	4.25
$12.51 to 25.00	3.50	4.50
$25.01 to 35.00	4.50	4.75
$35.01 to 60.00	5.50	5.25
$60.00 to 99.99	6.50	5.75
$100.00 and over	No Charge	

Rush shipping and Fourth Class are also available. Please call for details.

Subtotal

Sales Tax
California Destinations—add 7.75%.
Texas Destinations—add 8.25%.

Non-United States Residents
Australia and Europe: add 25%.
Other: Price +10% surface or 25% airmail.

Gift to Insight for Living
Tax-deductible in the United States.

Total Amount Due $
Please do not send cash.

Prices are subject to change without notice.

Payment by: ❑ Check or money order payable to Insight for Living or
❑ Visa   ❑ MasterCard   ❑ Discover Card   ❑ American Express   ❑ Bankcard
(In Australia)

Number

Expiration Date   /   Signature

We cannot process your credit card purchase without your signature

Name:

Address:

City: State:

Zip Code: Country:

Telephone: (   )   –   Radio Station:

If questions arise concerning your order, we may need to contact you.

Mail this order form to the Mail Center at one of these addresses:

Insight for Living
Post Office Box 69000, Anaheim, CA 92817-0900

Insight for Living, Inc.
GPO Box 2823 EE, Melbourne, VIC 3001, Australia

Order Form
Canadian Residents

(Residents of the United States, Australia, and other international locations,
please use order form on reverse side.)

GWYCS represents the entire *God's Word, God's World . . . and You* in a special album cover,
while GWY 1–5 are the individual tapes included in the series. GWY represents this study
guide, should you desire to order additional copies.

Product Code	Product Description	Qty.	Price	Total
GWY	Study Guide		$ 6.50	$.
GWYCS	Casette Series with study guide		37.25	.
GWY-	Individual cassette		7.48	.
GWY-	Individual cassette		7.48	.
GWY-	Individual cassette		7.48	.

			Subtotal	.
			Add 7% GST	.
			British Columbia Residents *Add 7% sales tax on individual tapes or cassette series.*	.
			Shipping *Shipping and Handling must be added. See chart for charges.*	.
			Gift to Insight for Living Ministries *Tax-deductible in Canada.*	.
			Total Amount Due $ *Please do not send cash.*	.

Amount of Order	Canada Post
Orders to $10.00	2.00
$10.01 to 30.00	3.50
$30.01 to 50.00	5.00
$50.01 to 99.99	7.00
$100 and over	No charge

Loomis Courier is also available.
Please call for details.

Prices are subject to change without notice.

Payment by: ❏ Cheque or money order payable to Insight for Living Ministries or
❏ Visa ❏ MasterCard

Number

Expiration Date / Signature

We cannot process your credit card purchase without your signature.

Name:

Address:

City: Province:

Postal Code: Country:

Telephone: ( ) – Radio Station:

If questions arise concerning your order, we may need to contact you.

Mail this order form to the Processing Services Department at the following address:

Insight for Living Ministries
Post Office Box 2510
Vancouver, BC, Canada V6B 3W7

Order Form
United States, Australia, and Other International Locations
(Canadian residents please use order form on reverse side.)

GWYCS represents the entire *God's Word, God's World . . . and You* series in a special album cover, while GWY 1–5 are the individual tapes included in the series. GWY represents this study guide, should you desire to order additional copies.

Product Code	Product Description	Qty.	Price	Total
GWY	Study Guide		$ 4.95	$.
GWYCS	Casette Series with study guide		25.95	.
GWY-	Individual cassette		6.00	.
GWY-	Individual cassette		6.00	.
GWY-	Individual cassette		6.00	.

	Order Total	.

Amount of Order	First Class	UPS
$ 7.50 and under	1.00	4.00
$ 7.51 to 12.50	1.50	4.25
$12.51 to 25.00	3.50	4.50
$25.01 to 35.00	4.50	4.75
$35.01 to 60.00	5.50	5.25
$60.00 to 99.99	6.50	5.75
$100.00 and over	No Charge	

Rush shipping and Fourth Class are also available. Please call for details.

UPS ❏   First Class ❏
Shipping and handling must be added.
See chart for charges.

Subtotal .

Sales Tax
California Destinations—add 7.75%.
Texas Destinations—add 8.25%. .

Non-United States Residents
Australia and Europe: add 25%.
Other: Price +10% surface or 25% airmail. .

Gift to Insight for Living
Tax-deductible in the United States. .

Total Amount Due $.
Please do not send cash.

Prices are subject to change without notice.

Payment by: ❏ Check or money order payable to Insight for Living or
❏ Visa   ❏ MasterCard   ❏ Discover Card   ❏ American Express   ❏ Bankcard (In Australia)

Number | | | | | | | | | | | | | | | |

Expiration Date | | / | | Signature | |
We cannot process your credit card purchase without your signature

Name: | | | | | | | | | | | | | | | | | | | | | | |
Address: | | | | | | | | | | | | | | | | | | | | | | |
City: | | | | | | | | | | | | | | | | State: | | | |
Zip Code: | | | | | Country: | | | | | | | | |
Telephone: (| | |) | | | – | | | | Radio Station: | | | |

If questions arise concerning your order, we may need to contact you.

Mail this order form to the Mail Center at one of these addresses:

Insight for Living
Post Office Box 69000, Anaheim, CA 92817-0900

Insight for Living, Inc.
GPO Box 2823 EE, Melbourne, VIC 3001, Australia

Order Form
Canadian Residents

(Residents of the United States, Australia, and other international locations, please use order form on reverse side.)

GWYCS represents the entire *God's Word, God's World . . . and You* in a special album cover, while GWY 1–5 are the individual tapes included in the series. GWY represents this study guide, should you desire to order additional copies.

Product Code	Product Description	Qty.	Price	Total
GWY	Study Guide		$ 6.50	$
GWYCS	Casette Series with study guide		37.25	
GWY-	Individual cassette		7.48	
GWY-	Individual cassette		7.48	
GWY-	Individual cassette		7.48	
			Subtotal	
			Add 7% GST	
			British Columbia Residents *Add 7% sales tax on individual tapes or cassette series.*	
			Shipping *Shipping and Handling must be added. See chart for charges.*	
			Gift to Insight for Living Ministries *Tax-deductible in Canada.*	
			Total Amount Due $ *Please do not send cash.*	

Amount of Order	Canada Post
Orders to $10.00	2.00
$10.01 to 30.00	3.50
$30.01 to 50.00	5.00
$50.01 to 99.99	7.00
$100 and over	No charge

Loomis Courier is also available. Please call for details.

Prices are subject to change without notice.

Payment by: ❏ Cheque or money order payable to Insight for Living Ministries or
❏ Visa   ❏ MasterCard

Number | | | | | | | | | | | | | | | | | |

Expiration Date | | | / | | | Signature |

We cannot process your credit card purchase without your signature.

Name: |
Address: |
City: | Province: |
Postal Code: | Country: |
Telephone: (| | |) | | | – | | | | Radio Station: |

If questions arise concerning your order, we may need to contact you.

Mail this order form to the Processing Services Department at the following address:

Insight for Living Ministries
Post Office Box 2510
Vancouver, BC, Canada V6B 3W7